THOUGHT
INCl

MW01169935

THOUGHTS ON THE UNIVERSE

INCLUDING EARTH

BY CURTIS W. IRION Ph.D

THOUGHTS ON THE UNIVERSE INCLUDING EARTH

DEDICATION
This and my other books would not have been possible without the
positive reinforcement given to me all of my life by my parents
William and Charlotte Irion

INTRODUCTION

I have been a very fortunate individual in having grown up in a secure educated household in a nice conservative town. Both of my parents worked in the field of education and still today are very active in the Presbyterian Church. My early upbringings were very church oriented and so I learned much about Biblical times. My father being a historian and a voracious reader must have transmitted some sort of special genes into me. I also love to read and all kinds of history are of a major interest. However, before you knew it I was in college studying biology and chemistry. I have taught these subjects for thirty-five years in both high school and college. When you teach both of these disciplines I guess it only makes sense that you are really into a blend of both subjects. In other words, I really like biochemistry and especially the nutritional aspects of this discipline. But as one ages perhaps it also makes sense to really try to understand the universe as a whole. At least this is true, as I understand it with my somewhat limited mind. So when you get into the whole universal concept it is only natural to me to understand the natural histories of our earth. So I read all kinds of history books and as time goes by I hope I am gaining somewhat of an insight into what's been going on for a long period of time. The universe is really old and we are just a speck in the whole show. Millions of stars have long ago exhausted their fuels and any planets orbiting them are also long gone. Perhaps some of these planets had some form of organic life that dwelled on them for millions of years. They are gone and lost to history. It should be easy to understand that we are far from being the center of the universe. However, we certainly do deal with our own realities and see existence in our own separate ways. So what I decided to do was to take a look at some thoughts dwelling in my brain from my studies and put some thoughts into a book. In a way these are just a bunch of essays that have been well researched and hopefully are accurate. When one reads a wide assortment of books hopefully a lot of thoughts come together and make sense. I have tried to add interesting thoughts for the reader of material one may find of interest. I decided to act like an uninformed student in that I have avoided the concept of the paragraph. It sort of allowed my mind to flow without all that English grammatical jumbo. Actually I like all of that jumbo but not this time. I also tried my best to avoid the Internet but of course every now and then Google came in quite handy when needed. When utilized I approached it with the idea that only good research would be added. I figured I might as well follow the entropy of the universe for a while. That of course is random disorder and that is the flow of this book. In other words you do not know what's next in the readings and that might keep things interesting.

THOUGHTS ON THE UNIVERSE INCLUDING EARTH

The universe as we know it has been around for about fourteen billion years. That of course is according to the cosmologists whose job it is to study this big old universe. They are pretty bright, highly educated individuals since studying cosmology certainly is not an easy task. Cosmology is essentially a branch of astronomy that deals with origin, structure, and space-time relationships of the universe. At least that is what the Merriam-Webster dictionary thinks of them as a whole. Right now they are trying to figure out if ours is the only universe or do others indeed exist? That's a tough one to call but perhaps by checking out a supernova study from 1996 we can at least reach a theoretical potential for other universes. Without getting too deep this study showed that the universe should not be accelerating as fast as it is. Edwin Hubble of course observed the acceleration of the universe in 1929. So what some cosmologists are currently thinking is that for the acceleration to occur at the pace it is then our universe must be part of a number of existing universes. Without getting into the math they believe it is possible that right after the Big Bang little bits of space might have pinched off of our universe forming other universes. That's pretty wild of course but certainly possible since existence does exist. Of course it is also possible to explain our universe's rate of expansion is due to gravity leaking out of some kinds of holes existing in weird universal places. Time perhaps may tell!

OBVIOUSLY HUMANS DO EXIST

Yep existence does exist as least as we know it. Humans became humans through a long evolutionary pathway and we became what are known as *Homo sapiens sapiens* somewhere around 200,000 years ago. We became modern humans and after awhile we were even given individual names. We got such names as Abraham, Jesus, Jimmy Buffet, and Mick Jagger just to name a few. Most of us are lost to the eternity of time but we do have very explicit records of a bunch of us. Probably a real character was Simon the Stylite. He hung around the earth in the 400's C.E. and was actually known by some as the "great wonder of the world". Of course not much was really known about the true world at that time but in his day and geographical area Christianity was a big thing. Monasteries were spread out in these areas around the Middle East and piety and self-denial were in fashion in some areas. Simon somewhere along the line got caught up with a concept that the Messalian sect of religious people thought was appropriate. They were into "Adam's sin" which could be thought of as an interesting concept. It was all about the idea that this sin has cast a demon on humans and not much could shake it off. Not even divine grace. Well actually they thought that long continual prayer might do the trick. Simon thought that concept to be pretty neat so at an early age joined a monastery and got into fasting. He even decided to tie a rope around his stomach so tightly that it ultimately cut into his body. This freaked out the monks and they told him he was no longer welcome. This was way too weird for them to imagine. So he then moved into a local village named Telanissos and decided to become a hermit. After some soul searching he decided to go on a 40 day fast with a twist. He wanted to seal his cottage with mud so that he could not escape if he lost control during the fast and bolted. The senior priest in the area said no way unless you place in the cottage 10 rolls of bread and a jug of water. He relented and fasted he did. After 40 days the religious people broke in and he was alive but barely conscious. According to legion no bread or water had been consumed but of course this would be a Guiness Book of Records thing since one cannot survive that long without water. Maybe the cottage leaked and while he was asleep water dripped into his mouth as he snored. Anyway he survived and things just got better and better. He moved to a local hilltop and started placing rocks on it forming a somewhat small pillar. Simon being a character of sorts then tied a 30-foot long chain to his ankle and tied the other end to a big rock on the pillar. He would stand there as long as possible chanting long prayer type things to the crowd that had started to get into vibes as such. This lasted for a while but when bugs started eating into his swollen ankles the local authorities made him remove the chain. Not to be deterred around 423 C.E. without taking anytime off he started to erect a big pillar. He was really deeply involved because in 423 the pillar stood 9 feet high but by 459 it reached a height of 54 feet. He was indeed aiming for heaven. He basically stood on top of this pillar for years continually bending over and then standing while constantly yelling out wild crazy prayers. Word got out on him and people from Arabia, Britain, Gaul, and Egypt flocked to watch his act. Many probably dug his style somewhat like some modern day Christians get into singing, chanting, and saying crazy nonsensical things. Talking in tongues could be added to this current scenario. He really got into it at Easter as he stood with his arms outstretched from sunset to dawn being constant with the loud prayer thing. Time moved on and his body steadily deteriorated with pus oozing out of nasty places. Incredibly he lived for 69 years but when he finally croaked his body was still standing as he slowly went into rigamortis. Some nice humans climbed up his personal tower and got him down to earth. It is not known where he was buried but it probably would have been nice to build a big pyramid for this unusual character.

ANOTHER FUNNY GUY

By moving up to the 20th century the universe has offered to us another special type of human. This guy was born in 1922 in the United States to fourth-generation German-American parents. He reached early adulthood at what was easily the most vicious time of human history. It could be called the time of "Adolf Hitler Madness" which of course was World War II. During the war he was attached with the 106th Infantry Division as an advanced scout. Unfortunately one day he advanced too far and was captured by the Germans and sent to the beautiful German city of Dresden. His name was Kurt Vonnegut Jr. and his Dresden experience certainly played a critical role in his life experience. Dresden with a rich history was exceptionally active between the years of 1697 to 1763. During this time period elaborate buildings were produced and it became an art-collecting city containing exceptional paintings. Even after World War I more architectural gems were produced until the National Socialists slowed down the show. Unfortunately worse was to come to Dresden and in January 1945 the Allies decided to try to totally wipe out certain German cities as this may aid in the Soviet advance into Germany. They picked Dresden and on February 13, 1945 the RAF Bomber Command sent 796 Auro Lancaster bombers and 9 De Havilland Mosquitoes over the city and they dropped 1,478 tons of high explosives and 1,182 tons of incendiaries onto the city. The next day the United States Air Force sent 311 B-17s to Dresden and they dropped 771 tons of explosives. Unfortunately for Vonnegut he was captured December 14, 1945 and so he was right in the city during the bombing. The allies had a pretty good idea as to what would happen since they understood the physics of "Fire-Bombing". It works something like this scenario. You first drop large amounts of high-explosive devices thereby blowing the roofs off of buildings thereby exposing the timbers of the buildings. Then you rain down the incendiary devices (fire-sticks) to ignite the open buildings and then finalize the insult with more high explosives. This creates a "fire-storm" with temperatures reaching 1500°F. This of course produces extremely hot air that rises rapidly above the city. Cold air then rushes in at the ground level from outside and this has the potential to suck the inhabitants into the fire. Well this nasty idea certainly worked since 15 square kilometers was devastated. This included the destruction of 14,000 houses, 72 schools, 22 hospitals, 19 churches, 5 theaters, 50 banks and insurance companies, 31 department stores, 31 large hospitals, and 62 administration buildings. Oh yes we probably should not forget the civilians. Most historians estimate that 30,000 – 50,000 died and untold thousands hurt in countless ways. Other people feel up to 135,000 died and even today the figures are difficult to gauge since countless refuges inhabited the city. All of these figures are of course horrendous but at least 2 wonderful cases of survival did occur. For one the magnificent treasures of the city were previously removed and therefore they survived to be seen once again by future generations. The other positive note is that Kurt Vonnegut was 3 stories down in a building. His prison cell happened to be an underground meat locker in the building known as Schachthof Funf (Slaughterhouse Five). He and 7 other prisoners survived but there were things to do when they surfaced out of their prison. They had to gather as many of the burned bodies as possible to be placed in a mass grave. This difficult work ended when the Nazis decided to just blast the bodies with blow torches since there were far too many for burial. The war soon ended and he was liberated and even received a purple heart that he later said was due to a case of "frostbite". Obviously the nastiness he witnessed had a profound affect on him and upon coming back to America he ultimately became a writer of books. His most famous was of course the book titled Slaughterhouse-Five, which was a personal and impersonal look at his world. Like his other well-known books like Cat's Cradle and Breakfast of Champions he tended to combine satire, dark humor, comedy, and compassion in a manner highly received by the intellects of society. His last book Timequake was a classic and a few quotes might be in order in no special order.

"Now imagine this: A man creates a hydrogen bomb for a paranoid Soviet Union, makes sure it will work, and then wins a Nobel Peace Prize! This real life-character, worthy of a story by Kilgore Trout, was the late physicist Andrei Sakharov. He won the Nobel in 1975 for demanding a halt to the testing of nuclear weapons. He, of course, had already used *his*. His wife was a pediatrician! What sort of person could perfect a hydrogen bomb while married to a child-care specialist? What sort of physician would stay with a mate that cracked?
"Anything interesting happen at work today, Honeybunch?"
"Yes. My bomb is going to work just great. And how are you doing with that kid with chicken pox?"

"I asked A.E. Hotchner, a friend and biographer of the late Ernest Hemingway, if Hemingway had ever shot a human being, not counting himself. Hotchner said, "No".

"I say in lectures in 1996 that fifty percent or more of American marriages go bust because most of us no longer have extended families. When you marry somebody now, all you get is one person. I say that when couples fight, it isn't about money, sex, or power. What they're really saying is, "You're not enough people!" Sigmund Freud said he didn't know what women want. They want a whole lot of people to talk to."

A final quote before death
"The only difference between Hitler and Bush is that Bush was elected." Kurt Vonnegut dies at the age of 84 on April 11, 2007. He accidentally had a fall in his Manhattan home and succumbed due to his brain injuries. "So it goes."

WHAT ARE HUMANS MADE OF

The obvious answer to that question is that we are made of the elemental components of the universe. Actually we are mostly made up of the elements carbon, hydrogen, nitrogen, oxygen, phosphorous, and sulfur. We also contain probably about 26 other elements depending on a number of factors. Of course we contain elements in small quantities such as copper, nickel, and magnesium, which allow our enzymes to function correctly. We have some fluorine in us from our toothpaste to harden the enamel on our teeth. We even contain some dubious elements such as mercury, lead, and cadmium which we take in from environmental insults. Out of the 92 naturally occurring elements we probably contain about 33 or one third of the natural elements. Where could these elements possibly have come from? Well, we are made of the star-stuff emitted from the destruction of other stars that burned out way before our solar system was formed. It goes something like this. The stars of the universe are actually suns and they come small, medium, and big. They are big giant gaseous concoctions made up of hydrogen gas, which are hot enough for fusion to occur. Fusion is the process where hydrogen atoms are forced into each other forming helium and a bit of energy is released in the process. On our sun every second about 600 million tons of hydrogen fuses into helium. Sound like a lot and it is but the internal temperature of the sun is 15 million degrees Fahrenheit! That makes a lot of heat for our earth to say the least. Of course it could get real hot since the temperature sometimes on Venus can reach 900°F. Of course it is closer to the Sun than us but its atmosphere is mostly carbon dioxide, which creates one big "Greenhouse Effect". Mercury is the closest planet to the Sun with very little atmosphere yet its temperature may only be about 450°F. "Greenhouse Effects can be costly. Anyway, our Sun has been around for about 4.5 billion years and is half way through it fusion cycle. So what will happen to it when it starts to cool down due to a lack of fuel? Well the answer to that question is that it will become a red giant. Essentially this means that as the hydrogen fuel is used up our Sun will shrink causing the center of it to become extremely hot. It will get so hot that the helium elements will fuse together forming all kinds of new elements such as beryllium. Beryllium for example can then combine with helium forming carbon. With more heat even bigger atoms such as iron and nickel will be formed. Finally as all the fuel is used up our sun will collapse and then become a super-hot red giant, which will then burst and send all of these new elements into the fabric of outer space. This process has been happening for billions of years to other stars and will continue for many more years. Obviously this is an interesting scenario but it does not explain the formation of all of the elements of the universe. Our sun and other small or medium sized stars can only produce around the first 28 elements and 92 natural ones exist. It is the big massive stars that produce the rest of the bigger elements. Massive stars burn their fuels at a very fast pace with some actually exhausting the fuels in as little as 100 million years. These stars upon their inward collapse get so hot that protons, neutrons, and electrons free themselves allowing the formation of these heavier elements. Finally a colossal explosion results called a supernovae and the contents from this star are sent millions of miles into outer space. This allows the formation of new suns and solar systems. This we believe is the case for our solar system which was formed from the leftovers of a massive star fairly close to our soon to be formed solar system. This haphazard event occurred in our area of the universe since a great cloud of gases and dust was in this vicinity. The magnitude of the supernovae explosion hurled the leftovers of this massive star at this cloud and caused it to collapse inward. The cloud slowly began to spin due to a law called the conservation of angular momentum. Over time the spinning rapidly increased and with the competing forces of gravity, gas pressure, and rotation, this massive cloud of gases, dust, and new elements flattened out into a spinning pancake shape. Of interest is that a bulge at the center existed which will become our sun. Of course the well-known magnetohydrodynamic effect came into play. Actually only known to some scientists this effect involves the idea that magnetic effects can induce currents in a moving conductive plasma fluid. This allowed the central bulge to not push out of the pancake shape but instead it moved towards the outer part of the pancake shape. Finally over a time period of about 10 million years various instabilities in the entire rotating pancake cloud caused localized regions to begin to contract gravitationally forming the sun and the planets. This certainly makes sense as the orbits of the planets lie nearly in a plane with the sun at the center. They also revolve in the same direction and mostly rotate in the same direction. The new earth contained the 92 naturally occurring elements with an iron-nickel core. The lighter elements hung around near the surface of the earth and we are made up mostly of these lighter ones. So it goes.

WHAT GREENHOUSE EFFECT

It sure is cold out in the depths of outer space. Is it as cold as absolute zero? Well temperature is actually a measurement of how fast atoms are moving. That is a reflection of how fast they are moving. Absolute zero is minus 459.67°F and that is the temperature where there is no heat energy remaining to be extracted from an element. All subatomic particles stop motion at this temperature. Physicists say we can never reach that temperature. Nevertheless deepest outer space has a temperature of minus 455°F, which is pretty darn cold. Minus 129°F is the coldest we have been able to reach on earth as long as records have been kept. Actually that is not a true statement since in the modern world of science we have been able to obtain a temperature of 810 trillionths of a degree F above absolute zero. This occurred at the Massachusetts Institute of Technology in Cambridge and this feat even made it into the 2008 Guiness World's Records book. The Nobel Peace Prize winner Wolfgamg Ketterle directed this accomplishment using laser beams to slow down a small cloud of sodium atoms trapped in place with magnets. He was working on producing a new form of matter called a Bose-Einstein condensate (BEC). Both Albert Einstein and an Indian physicist Satyendra Bose theorized in 1925 that if we subject atoms to a temperature near absolute zero then these atoms would not function as a solid, liquid, or gas. Instead a group of a few million of them would enter the same quantum state and behave as one, which is the BEC. They actually have been produced since 1995 and Ketterle is continuing an advanced study of them, which may ultimately lead to remarkable new events taking shape. He is hoping that his studies of BECs may lead to new forms of matter that may function as superconductors at room temperatures. This may ultimately lead to new and better energy sources for the future. The heck we say with crude oil as the ultimate fuel for the world. Of an added note BECs may some day function to improve the processing speed of computers and may even provide new ways to store information.

WHY DO WE COME IN DIFFERENT COLORS

Homo Sapiens Sapiens evolved from an older primate line, which will be further discussed in a later section. The last branching off occurred about 5 million years ago when the chimps diverged away from the primates who ultimately became humans. We could call this group the primitive hominids. At this time period these two groups had many things in common. For one their skin was fair in complexion and they both had a small number of sweat glands. Both were also very hairy. Both groups also lived in the heavily forested areas of Africa. Now let's zoom up to 200,000 years ago when humans were now actually humans and chimps were still chimps. The genetics of the chimps changed little and they stayed in the forests of Africa. However, through millions of years of time the primitive hominids slowly left the forests and traveled to the East African savanna, which was quite, hot and dry. High amounts of ultraviolet light blasted into these primitive hominids for many years. This created a big problem which slowly but surely was conquered with natural selection. These hominids in order to survive now had to stay longer in the sun in order to get enough food to eat. The dense rich forests of Africa contained many more roots, leaves, and bugs, which were so much depended upon at that time period. Mammal brains do not like too much heat so it is likely that many hominids perished due to heatstroke. But genetic mutations most certainly occur and through time more and more hominids were born with more sweat glands. Over time these were the survivors of the savannas and modern humans now possess about 2 million sweat glands. Chimps still just have them mostly on the palms of their hands and the bottoms of their feet. Another positive mutation occurred over the millions of years after the chimps left us. Hominids were slowly losing their hairy bodies thereby exposing the skin to the intense heat of Africa. Their skin was getting scorched and that certainly was not fun. To further complicate the story the intense sunlight was destroying their folic acid levels, which is a B vitamin. Folic acid is needed by mammals for many enzymatic cellular reactions and is needed to insure adequate red blood cell production. It is needed for DNA production, which involves our genes and the proteins we produce. It is especially needed for many complex reactions involving a developing baby. Lack of adequate levels of it during pregnancy can cause a number of birth defects. Once again genetics came to the rescue by slowly changing the skin color of the primitive hominids. Primate skin contains pigment-producing cells known as melanocytes. Inside of these cells are areas known as melanosomes, which produce the dark pigment known as melanin. The melanosomes are actively transported to the outer layer of primate skin called basal keratinocytes. The more melanosome activity the darker the skin color. Over a long time period genetic evolutionary changes occurred to certain areas of the DNA of some hominids causing them to be able to produce more enzymatic production in their melanosomes. They got bigger, more numerous, and contained more melanin. These individuals slowly became darker which gave them a great evolutionary advantage. They had less folic acid breakdown and could stay out in the heat for longer periods of time increasing their rate of survival. Their offspring inherited the darker skin and over many years the hominids of Africa took on a dark coloration. Lighter skinned individuals tended not to survive as readily as those with the good dark skin. The darker skinned individuals could forage for longer periods of time and the females were better able to feed their offspring. However, this is not the end of the story since another most important vitamin comes into play when we deal with primate skin. It is needed for making good bones and is most certainly involved in maintaining a healthy immune system. Our skin is able to make it from cholesterol, which is found in skin cells. When ultraviolet B rays shine on our skin vitamin D is made which is then activated in our liver and kidneys. Primitive hominids needed it and so do we as modern humans. Vitamin D will be more readily discussed later in this book. Anyway having dark skin was of an obvious benefit but did this high amount of melanin inhibit their abilities to produce optimal levels of vitamin D? The answer is a big no! These hominids hung out in the savannas naked as a jaybird and the intense sunlight allowed them to make around 10,000 IUs per day, which certainly helped them in keeping strong bones and a healthy immune system. But as modern humans came about we started to migrate out of this area of Africa and slowly explore the world. Thousands of years ago various small migrations moved through the Middle East towards Asia and onward. Other small groups over the years moved more northward out of Africa moving into Europe. Through certain genetic changes still not known the Asian populations slowly developed somewhat of a lighter skin color. Selective pressures certainly were of some influence. In the more northern areas of Europe the lack of intense sunlight played a major role in skin color changes. It is pretty obvious that the climate in many areas of Europe differs drastically from Africa. The sun is not as intense and often the days are cloudy. The season's change and the darkness patterns of winter set in as they have for many years. Humans had to adapt and one adaptation was to wear animal hides. In other words, clothing became quite popular. Many humans readily adapted and yet for some the climatic changes were harder to deal with. The plant type food sources varied and animal foods were needed for survival. However the lack of optimal levels of sunshine became a major issue for survival. As previously noted humans need adequate amounts of vitamin D for healthy bone structure and for a well-rounded immune system. The summer would allow them to shed clothes and make this vitamin from the sun whenever there were few clouds. Unfortunately, from late fall until spring the ability to make vitamin D was almost impossible and the small amount stored in their livers was rapidly depleted. The animals on the European continent did not provide vitamin D. It is true that cold-water ocean fish contain it but these folks were not big time fishermen. Natural selection once again slowly took hold. It has now been shown that a genetic mutation occurred to a certain gene known as SLC24A5. This gene is involved in how much melanin is made in melanocytes. It should be noted that light and dark-skinned humans typically have close to the same amount of melanocytes. So the mutation of this gene caused individuals who carry it to actually produce much less melanin. This slowly over time was a positive factor for these early Europeans since those that carried it had a lighter skin tone. This allowed them to produce much more vitamin D in the summer and more to be stored in the liver for the winter months. These individuals carrying this genetic mutation therefore had a greater chance to survive and reproduce. They and their offspring possessed a stronger bone system and also a better immune system. As a result the population of early Europe slowly became much lighter in color. Of a final note it is interesting to note that small groups of individuals left areas of Asia and moved to the extremes of the north. They became the Eskimos such as the Inuits and the Lapps. They maintained as they do today a brownish type skin, which one would think, would be a negative survival factor. After all it is cold and dark in the north and they wore plenty of clothes. It is their diet that has helped them survive. They live partly off of the animals of the ocean such as fish, walrus, and seals. These food sources are all very high in vitamin D, which they have gotten from the northern food chains. Sunlight is not a major factor in their survival.

THE HOMINID ADVENTURE

It is now time to go back to about 56 million years ago where the earliest primitive primate has now been found. These small mice sized primates were recently found in Yellowstone National Park and are called plesiadapiforms. Through millions of years time evolution changed the primate line in many ways producing all kinds of interesting primate species. Most of these died out but certain ones survived and developed larger bodies and better survival structures. They developed somewhat large brains, enhanced vision with the eyes facing forward, and specialized hands and feet for grasping all kinds of things. Moving onwards to about 25 - 30 million years ago the primitive primates had reached a monkey-like ape look. Somewhere during this time period, the remaining primates essentially separated into two distinct groups. One group through evolutionary changes became the old world and new world monkeys. The old world ones hung out basically around Africa and the new world monkeys somehow made it to South America. The other group, which underwent this separation, had a more ape-like appearance and various branches occurred from this line. About 17 million years ago the gibbons separated from the main group. The orangutans took off about 12 million years ago. A big separation occurred 6-8 million years ago when the gorillas branched away from the chimp-like primates. Finally as already noted somewhere around 5 million years or so ago the chimps and the pre-humans separated into different pathways. This now brings us ultimately to our modern line. The total pathway is far from complete but fossilized evidence and a bunch of really intelligent scientists are putting the puzzle together. The earliest hominid fossil found along this new line belongs to *Ardipithecus ramidus*. Dated to about 4.3 million years ago it was a small rather chimp-like creature. But it was different from the chimp and most likely other primitive- hominids roamed around at that time period trying to be the best at natural selection. Nobody knows what happened to those creatures but around 4 million years ago we found a totally new creature known as *Australopithecus anamensis*. Although still very much chimp-like with a small brain it was bipedal and had different types of teeth. Actually a number of *Australopithecus* species existed at the same time in Africa. The number was probably around one dozen and it is interesting to note that a number of hominid types were fighting for evolutionary survival for a couple million years in Africa. Most of these species died out for unknown reasons. They still had small brains ranging from about 400 –500 ccs. Lots of big African wild animals probably did not help much. However, some survived and around 2.4 million years ago a type of early *Homo* species emerged. It is possible they were decedents of some type of *Australopithecus* but we do not know for sure. They had *Australopithecus* looks in many ways but a bigger brain. The brain of *Homo habilis* was in the vicinity of 640 ccs and probably used primitive stone tools. *Australopithecus* species were still hanging out in the savannas when *Homo* came about but their time for existence on the earth was due to expire. *Homo habilis* may not have been the only *Homo* species found at this time period but for now it is the only species found. They hung out in Africa from about 2.4-1.5 million years ago. They were very ape-like but about 5 foot tall for the males and had hands that more closely resembled modern humans. Their tools were pretty much chipped rocks used for digging up roots and bugs. On occasion they probably found them useful for digging through the thick skin of some dead animal. Nobody is exactly sure but around 1.8 million years ago another primate entered the scene. It was known as *Homo erectus* and science does not know if it evolved from *habilis* or from another close primate line. But we do know that it was pretty smart for that time period anyway. This species made it until about 300,000 years ago. It had a fairly big brain between 900 ccs to 1200ccs. It was capable of some sort of rudimentary speech and its stone tools were more advanced. We believe it had some ability to cook with fire. We are not entirely sure about the fire thing. Actually the first real evidence of a group of pre-humans continually using a fire pit for food has been found in Zhoukoudian, China. It is estimated this pit existed between 550,000 – 450,000 years ago. It was probably made by a group of *Homo erectus*. Anyway due to factors unknown small groups of *Homo erectus* decided to migrate out of Africa first going to Asia and then to Europe. The actual times are still being debated but for thousands upon thousands of years various groups of *Homo erectus* slowly worked there way to parts unknown. As they settled in various areas minute genetic changes occurred to individual populations. Some changes were for the good and some worsened their survival. Unfortunately for them they all failed to make it as a dominant species on earth. They were destined to just leave us with a bunch of difficult fossilized records to evaluate. However, it appears that a group of *Homo erectus* creatures in Africa contained the necessary evolutionary genes putting them in a direct pathway for modern humans. Once again through thousands of year's time, they changed and became known as archaic *Homo sapiens*. They were better equipped with bigger brains and the ability to hunt, survive, and care for their offspring. Their superior genes were passed on and better ones developed and by about 200,000 years ago this group took on the role of modern humans. They became *Homo sapien sapiens*. They were still pretty primitive as far as brain usage but by about 100,000 years ago small groups slowly left Africa and in the year 2008 there are over 6.5 billion of them on earth. That is the end of that story for now.

WHAT IS UP WITH OUR BIG BRAINS?

It should be pretty obvious that our brain is bigger than a chimp brain. In fact it is actually about 3 times larger than we would expect from a typical primate of our size. The chimp, our closest genetic relative has an average brain size of 420 ccs. Typically we humans average about 1300 – 1400 and some may even go up to 2000 ccs. Brain size is not necessarily a big deal about intelligence. Albert Einstein was a fairly bright guy and his size was smaller than the average human brain. But more will be written about him later. Of course some mammals have really big brains. Sperm whales are pretty smart and they have a brain size average of 7,800 ccs. In American terms this comes out to 17 pounds of brain. Of course they are pretty big characters. Your beagle's brain is about 72 ccs. No wonder they do not always listen to you! Actually dogs have a potentially magnificent brain. We as humans have about 100 billion brain neurons, which seems like an awful lot. Yet the lowly octopus has around 300 million. We also have about 12 million cells allowing us to smell but the dog has about 1 billion. The lazy bloodhound has about 4 billion. No wonder it is used for smelling out all kinds of things. Anyway, 200,000 years ago humans were pretty much anatomically correct as we are today. But we were still pretty darn primitive. We may have learned to hunt and maintain small groups better but we were far from being able to do chemistry stoichiometrical problems. Evolutionary changes must have occurred leading to a smarter brain. Today even with brilliant scientists we are just now learning some of the adjustments the brain made in order for us to become smarter and smarter. However, it is most likely that the first groups of humans who left Africa already had some unique gene changes, which gave them a better ability to coordinate their brain activities. As time went on some humans underwent other positive gene changes furthering our intelligence. For example animals contain a gene known as HAR1, which is found from birds to mammals and did not change much for 310 million years. However since we branched from the chimps it has changed 18 times. This gene really turns on from the 7th to 9th week of human gestation stimulating brain growth. It is also thought to play a major role in the development of the outer brain cortex, which is the gray matter of the brain. Gray matter contains billions of brain connections and is one of the reasons we are humans. We are fairly confident that HAR1 is a major factor in the production of the 6 layers of neurons in the brain's cortex. Other genes have been implicated in the advancement of the human condition. For example the gene PDYN codes for the making of certain proteins that allow brain neurons to produce differing levels of various nerve chemicals involved in perception, behavior, and memory. This gene is highly active in humans. Oxytocin is a hormone that most females use in labor and lactation. Both males and females use it in the brain and it is associated with promoting trust in other people. A higher activation of it in humans may have led us to work better in small hunting and gathering groups. A favorite gene now receiving lots of research is FOXP2. This gene has been found in mammals for millions of years undergoing few mutations. However it has indeed mutated, as we slowly became humans. This gene has allowed us to produce various proteins in differing amounts by turning on other genes. FOXP2 is heavily involved during embryonic growth activating unknown genes that play an important role in the development of the speech area of the brain. Much more needs to be understood as to the total mechanisms involved but the ability to speak most certainly played a big role in human advancement. Finally we should note that a major advancement of the human brain occurred to our prefrontal cortex. Located behind our forehead it has enlarged two times as big as expected. It is considered to be the area where the conductor of an orchestra would be located. It sends out signals to other parts of the brain just as the conductor would at specific times during a concert. It tends to send signals to certain areas allowing us to develop our interests and maturities. Our gifted areas receive high stimulations and by the time we are in our mid-twenties we tend to have formed the necessary patterns and ideas, which will guide us through our path in life.

TRIAL AND ERROR

I wonder what it was like being an early human being. They had to drink water and eat interesting foodstuffs to survive. It was probably pretty hard to kill most living animals. On occasion they probably found some nasty semi-decomposed animal to thrive on. Of course standard fair would have included insects and worms, which are up to 70% protein, which was great for the digestion and growth. That is actually better than a hot dog, which is about 18% protein. Anyway fruits, nuts, seeds, and roots were also a likely addition to their daily diet. In general plants can be a very high nutritional source and even the leaves contain useful minerals and vitamins. I am quite sure that over the years countless different plants were investigated for their eating potentials. Unfortunately in many cases this involved trial and error. An error could become a problem during those early years. Although most plants are edible many are indeed poisonous. For example when early humans traveled around the Mediterranean they would have encountered the common oleander plant (*Nerium oleander*). This common perennial evergreen shrub has small leaves and very fragrant flowers. It is also one of the most poisonous of plants including all of its parts. The milky saps of the stems are particularly poisonous containing toxic cardiac glycosides. The leaves are also poisonous and eating 10 or so of them might cause death. Poisoning would be nasty starting with the vomiting, nausea, and diarrhea. Tremors, seizures, and coma may follow. Then the heart kicks in and goes into cardiac shock with the result often being death. It still on occasion causes death in grazing animals. Well early humans probably did not know that but until the word got out it is possible a number of early travelers met their demise from that plant. Even during World War II soldiers were poisoned by cooking their hot dogs, using oleander twigs over a fire. Even fungi may have taken their toll on early humans. The death cap mushroom (*Amanita phalloides*) is a common all white mushroom found throughout the world. Throughout time it has led to the demise of many humans. It happens to contain a number of cyclopeptides such as amatotoxins and fallotoxins. About 5 – 12 hours after eating a good size one or so (50 grams) the individual first gets vomiting and nausea. These poisons travel to the liver and then destroy it within 24 hours. Today if you are lucky and near a good hospital you may get a quick liver transplant. Even so today you mostly die and that certainly was the case for the first few people to eat that mushroom. Live and learn was what must have been accomplished. Now of course not all poisonous plants will kill you. Native Americans arrived in the Eastern United States somewhere around 14,000 years ago. We actually now know this by studying the DNA found in fossilized human feces (coprolites) found in a cave in Oregon. Anyway they had to try out the local plants. They could not totally live off of animals even though dog protein was also found in these feces. One of the first plants to emerge in the spring in large numbers is skunk cabbage (*Symplocarpus foetidus*). This big plant looks like a large purple cabbage and grows in wet areas of the forests. I would like to think that these Native Americans would be tempted to taste it after a long winter. I am sure they did at some point. However, they soon found out about 2 unpleasant problems. One problem was whenever they cut the leaf it smelled like skunk pee. Once they got over that when they took a bite of the leaf it felt like sharp painful needles were poking into their mouth, tongue, and throat. This feeling lasted possibly for hours. They did not know it at the time but the leaves contain loads of calcium oxalate molecules that were causing their distress. One bite was enough and they soon recovered but they soon learned this was an unpleasant plant to eat. To give these adventurers some special credit they did learn for survival that boiling the leaves in 2 changes of water would remove the poisons. They then could safely eat the leaves even though most of the nutrients were now lost. Not all of the explorations of plant tasting led to a poisonous outcome. Many plants found to be acceptable to early humans actually possessed many medicinal powers. Even today we are still using many of these plants for their health and healing powers. When humans moved into the Mediterranean region they ultimately discovered the common sage (*Salvia officinalis*). Nobody knows when it was first used but today this common herb is used all over the world. It is added to all kinds of meats and soups. It is a common perennial grown in gardens throughout the world and it contains soft, gray-green fragrant leaves. Martin Luther once said: "Why should a man die whilst sage grows in his garden?" Now nobody knows when humans first cultivated common sage but the early humans may actually have found out that this common herb possessed magical healing powers. Perhaps they boiled the leaves and took the extract and added it to wounds or other skin problems. Before they regularly used fire they may have just crushed the leaves and applied the juices to their wounds. Most likely in many cases adding the juice to the wounds etc may have actually caused them to heal. They certainly had no clue but we now know common sage leaves contain ursolic acid, which is a great anti-inflammatory agent. Try it today for wounds and other areas of inflammation. It works as well today as it did thousands of years ago. Common sage also contains a host of other chemicals that make it a great medicinal plant. Seeping the leaves in boiling water brings out a number of essential oils and tannin-like chemicals out of the leaves. One of these chemicals is known as thujone and it is known to kill both bacteria and viruses. Applying the boiled extract to *Staph*-containing boils should kill the bacteria after a certain number of applications. I think the best use for sage though is when one has a sore throat. The common remedy of course is to gargle with saltwater which actually does very little to remedy the situation. However it is now known that gargling with sage tea is the best way to cure a sore throat. All one has to do is boil the leaves and gargle as often as possible with the tea drink. The thujone along with other chemicals inhibit, and kills the viruses or bacteria, which are causing the infection. I wonder when early humans found out that neat trick.

THE CELL

The typical human is made of about a trillion cells or so. Many of them are actually bacteria and other parasite type things that are just hanging out with us for one reason or another. All of our cells are considered to be eukaryotic types versus the bacteria, which are prokaryotic in nature. We have evidence that the first extremely primitive cells evolved around 3.5 billion years or so ago. Sedimentary rocks dated to that long ago have been shown to contain fossil stromatolites, which appear to be primitive colonies of singled celled bacteria-like organisms. It is possible that more modern bacteria and even photosynthetic bacteria evolved in a complicated manner from these early primitive strains. It certainly must have been a very slow road to these early cells especially since there was no atmospheric oxygen present during their quest for becoming a primitive cell. A tremendous amount of ultraviolet rays were hitting the oceans since there was no protective ozone layer above the earth. However the early primitive cells did appear probably somewhat at a level in the ocean allowing for their survival. Somewhere along the line the photosynthetic bacteria evolved and utilizing the concept of photosynthesis slowly started to fill the atmosphere with oxygen. During photosynthesis carbon dioxide in the bacterial cell combined with water to produce glucose sugar and oxygen. Much more oxygen was produced by these cells than was needed, and so slowly over millions of years time our atmosphere started to contain substantial amounts of oxygen. Some of these oxygen molecules made it high up in our atmosphere where they were blasted by ultraviolet rays. This produced a chemical reaction forming O_3 molecules commonly called ozone. Once again very slowly the protective ozone layer was formed which protects our cells from excessive ultraviolet rays damage. Over time then a number of different cellular entities existed in the oceans utilizing different methods for energy production. These cells contained DNA, which allowed for the production of many different types of proteins to be produced in the cells. DNA is essentially a blueprint that codes for protein making. That is the major function of all cells. Cells are really protein making factories. The proteins produced serve as the bodily parts of the cells. They are also involved in transmissions that occur in the cells. In fact, a whole slew of reactions involving proteins occur continually in cells. The DNA contains the code for making all of the proteins of a particular cell. Specifically the code is contained in the genes that are found in the DNA. When a gene turns on it sends a message into a specific area of the cell known as the ribosomes. In the ribosome amino acids are connected to each other making specific proteins. Twenty-two amino acids occur in nature and the genes contain the information for putting them in a logical order for each particular protein. Early primitive cells had to have this DNA mechanism to survive yet they still were far from the complexities of modern cells. Finally about 2 billlion years ago the somewhat rapid development of complex cells came to fruition. Of course nobody absolutely knows the exact developments, which occurred, but most scientists would currently bet on the "Endosymbiotic Theory". This theory pretty much involves 3 primitive cells, which actually became 1 more complex cell. During this time period our atmosphere contained adequate amounts of oxygen from millions of years of production by the more primitive photosynthetic bacteria. This theory suggests that a fairly large primitive cell existed along with two other smaller cells that possessed some highly unusual characteristics. One of the smaller cells is called a mitochondria and it contained DNA along with 37 genes. What is unique about it is that mitochondria had developed a method using oxygen and glucose to produce copious amounts of energy. The other small cell is called a chloroplast and it also contains DNA. What is unique about it is that it is actually a photosynthetic machine in that it could take large amounts of carbon dioxide and combine it with water. This allowed it to produce lots of glucose and oxygen just like the primitive photosynthetic bacteria. The "Endosymbiotic Theory" believes these 2 smaller cells somehow fused into the larger more primitive cell ultimately allowing a great evolutionary adaptation to occur. The larger cell was able to take the energy produced by the mitochondrial cell to make huge amounts of energy in its cell. The chloroplast produced lots of glucose and oxygen, which fed the entire newly, formed cell and provided the large amount of oxygen needed for the mitochondria to make energy. This possible scenario led to the now advanced eukaryotic cells found in modern plants and animals. Of course this makes sense in the plant kingdom since plant cells do contain both mitochondria and chloroplasts. It is much more difficult to understand how the animal cells came about since they do not contain chloroplasts. Perhaps it is possible that some of the larger primitive cells only acquired the mitochondria and these over time would become primitive animal cells. Once again all of this is only a theory subject to much analysis by scientists but the plausibility exists that this is how the more modern cells were produced over many years of complex cellular changes.

WHY DID JRR TOLKIEN NOT USE DOGS

Without a doubt the dog (*Canus lupus familiaris*) is the human's buddy. Tolkien in his fascinating trilogy, "The Lord of the Rings" had all kinds of crazy critters in his saga about getting rid of the ring that was necessary so that evil did not rule the world of Middle Earth. Hobbits, humans, dwarfs, elves, wizards and Rangers were the standards of the day and this incredible journey also included various animals such as horses. But no dogs participated in this saga. I would bet it was because they barked too much and would ruin the show. They would have been caught in their journey and the bad wizard would have won. Evil would have reined and that just is not right. Anyway the dog sure does exist in today's somewhat evil world. In fact currently over 400 described breeds exist. Well over 152 of these breeds are currently recognized by the American Kennel Club. The different appearances are amazing but it should be noted that most of the breeds have only existed for the last 200 years. Even so, European paintings from the 1500s clearly show spaniels, mastiffs, hounds, and pointers. There must have been some early animal geneticists around back then. But the real question is where did dogs come from anyway? Well that actually is a tough one to call. Dogs are really carnivores and this line of mammals came about 40 – 50 million years ago. Specifically the canids of which the dog has descended from branched off from other carnivore families about 10 million years ago. All of the *Canis* species have an interesting thing about their chromosome number. They all possess 78 chromosomes in the nucleus of their cells. This includes the gray wolf (*Canis lupus*) and the dog. For many years it was somewhat accepted that the dog actually came about by basically domesticating some docile gray wolves. This domestication was thought to have occurred either in Asia or Europe. The earliest fossilized record of dogs is about 14,000 years ago. Presumably early wanderers took docile-like wolves and then slowly by continually keeping the most docile pups, produced the ancient dog line. In fact it is common knowledge that for years we thought dogs came from the gray wolf. However, new research is challenging this theory. Dogs actually possess a 30% smaller brain size than is found in the gray wolf. Their brain structure actually more resembles that of coyotes or jackals. But we do not believe they evolved from either of these two canids since the DNA is too different. It should also be noted that they possess a different teeth structure. Even their diet and tracks are much different from the gray wolf. It quite possibly would have been very difficult to domesticate the gray wolf. They very much resist human directions. They are extremely food possessive and need a high protein diet. They probably would have chased down, killed, and eaten the game that the early humans would be trying to kill for themselves. Even young wolf pups would have been hard to handle. From a genetic perspective certain gene sequences show that actually the wolf and the dog should have branched away from each other 76,000 – 135,000 years ago. If this is true then really primitive hunter-gathers moving about Europe during that time frame would have been too elemental in their knowledge of this huge undertaking. It actually might make more sense to see the development of the dog from a different type of wolf. Investigations are currently underway to see if the dog actually descended from the extinct *Canis lupus variabilis*. Fossilized remains of this small wolf have been found in China where it existed 100,000 to 200,000 years ago. Fossils show this wolf had more of a dog-type muzzle and dog-like teeth. It is possible that this was also a much more docile creature with a more omnivorous diet found in modern dogs. It certainly is possible that this animal tagged along with early wanderers and they slowly took the more mellow ones and developed them into the primitive dog species. Remember that humans spent thousands of years wandering about and so it is certainly possible that this small wolf led to our family friend. But how in the world have we been able to produce such a wild diversity of modern dogs? The answer of course lies in selective breeding using a relatively small amount of male dogs containing certain characteristics. They then bred these males with a larger number of females each having their own genetic characteristics. Over many generations all sorts of interesting creatures have been produced. Of course most of this was done before the advent of modern DNA genetics. For example we now know that one of the reasons we have some really small breeds is partly due to a recessive gene, which codes for the production of a protein known as insulin-like growth factor. This is a master growth regulator gene found on chromosome 15 and dogs that carry two of these genes only produce small amounts of insulin-like growth factor. They just stay little and this recessive gene has been around for at least 10,000 years since we know terriers were running around by then. By the way wolves do not have this recessive gene.

WHAT'S THE STUFF INSIDE AN ELEMENT

Elementary school kids should know that an element contains positively charged protons, neutrally charged neutrons, and teeny tiny negatively charged electrons. But what are they actually made up of? Well one would think that is pretty hard to say since these chemical structures are very small. In fact the mass of a proton has been found to be 1.67262×10^{-24} grams. The mass of the neutron is 1.67493×10^{-24} grams. To top it off the minute mass of the electron, which is part wave and part particle, is only 9.10939×10^{-28} grams. To put that into perspective the mass of the electron is so small that when we decide the masses of the different elements we do not even add the electron masses. What is mind blowing is that these masses were proven before the 1920's! Further advanced research into sub-nuclear chemistry has actually shown what makes up the protons and neutrons. They are made up of what are called quarks, which are again extremely small and contain differing masses and spins. They come in different weird names called flavors. We have in the universe so far the up, down, strange, charm, bottom, and top quarks. Protons are made up of 2 up and 1 down quark. The neutron contains 2 down and 1 up quark. They are held together by strong force gluons, which also have mass and they stream between the quarks holding them together forming protons and neutrons. Once again this has been shown to be factual stuff. What is not factual but intriguing is that physicists theorize that quarks are made up of the fundamental particles of nature called superstrings. These may consist of tiny filaments of energy that are some hundred billion billion times smaller that a single nucleus of an element. They possibly vibrate in different patterns thereby producing different particle properties. For example 1 string may vibrate in such a way that it would give it the mass and electrical charge of an electron. Another one might vibrate in such a way leading to quark-like properties. Again this is highly theoretical but perhaps we may have the answer. Going into operation sometime in 2008 the Large Hadron Collider may solve the question of superstrings and many other complex ideas in cosmology. On the other hand it may send physicists into a tale-spin starting back in many cases at square one. Built underlying the border between Switzerland and France it will send subatomic particles such as protons at 99.9999991 % the speed of light down a 17-mile tunnel and smash them up. By the way the speed of light is 670 million miles an hour or 186,000 miles per second. The collider is so complicated it will rival the Manhatten Project, which built the atomic bomb. Is it worth the price of 7 billion dollars? Well we may ultimately find out why the Big Bang created a universe containing more matter than antimatter. That surely must be worth the cost!

WHY THE UNIVERSE CONTAINS MASS

We will later on explain the concept of the Big Bang theory held in esteem by most scientists. But once again, existence exists so we may as well try to understand the science of it all. Mass and weight are 2 interesting concepts and of course gravity plays a big part. We weigh less on the moon than on earth but our mass is the same on both pieces of rock. So why do objects contain mass in the first place? The answer may lie at the disposal of the Large Hadron Collider or perhaps with the Big Bang itself. It all is about something called the Higgs Field or the Higgs Ocean. From the standpoint of the Big Bang, it is postulated that at the beginning of universal existence all of the potential energy of the universe was contained inside of an area billions of times smaller than a dot. Pretty wild but then a major explosion type expansion occurred producing in milliseconds the basic constituent particles making up the universe. Within seconds all kinds of fields and forces were produced. These include the strong and weak force and the electromagnetic force. It is possible that what was also produced which filled up the entire expanding universe was a field known as the Higgs Field (Higgs Ocean). Named after the famous Scottish Peter Higgs, who theorized its existence 40 years ago. This highly theoretical field resists the forward motions of essentially all of the known particles of the universe that contain mass. These would include possibly superstrings and the quarks. The basic idea is that the Higgs Field serves to decelerate the forward motion of these particles thereby giving them mass. Perhaps a way to think about is to pretend you are a major league baseball pitcher. When you throw the ball to home plate your arm encounters resistance and this is sort of like a bunch of quarks etc being slightly pushed back by the Higgs Field. Forget about gravity for now about that concept. This is actually a major theory of particle physics and soon we may have an answer as to whether it really exists. A major undertaking for the Large Hadron Collider is to smash up elements and to find out if the Higgs Field or Higgs particles actually exist. It is now theorized that a Higgs particle may be up to 100 - 200 times the size of a proton and will be observable if they are what we think they are. If we find they do not exist then a major change in particle physics will need to occur and many years of complex thought by very smart people will have to be reevaluated.

RELIGIOUS THOUGHTS

Nobody really knows when humans first started thinking about a higher consciousness. Is the universe just some crazy entity which just sort of happened and that's the way it is. Or is it possible that forces or something outside of our abilities to understand are involved in the crazy thing we call life? This is pretty serious stuff and humans somewhere along the line thought of the afterlife. We have found graves in Europe dated to 80,000 years ago, which contain tools, jewelry, and flowers. That probably can be deduced as some sort of afterlife type stuff. Most certainly early humans developed various religious type rites even when they were hunter-gathers moving about the continents. However, it really was when we started to settle down into so-called villages that we really got into the idea of religion. Supposedly one of the first establishments was in Jericho,

which is located 5 miles west of the Jordan River. Currently this is
Palestine territory. It is also located about 6 miles north of the Dead
Sea. It is dead in the way that it is so loaded with mineral salts that
typical plant and animal life cannot survive. We can say just a bunch
of weird bacteria in that sea. Anyway it was a nice place to settle
down. This area just happened to have a great spring of pretty pure
water, which never ran dry. It appears that right around the end of the
last ice age (11,000 B.C.E. – 10,000 B.C.E.) a group of people known
as Natufians tried to settle in this area. They stuck it out off and on
for a while but a cold spell of 200 years occurred around 10,000 years
ago and they wandered off to other areas. About 8000 B.C.E. a group
known as Pre-Pottery Neolithic A peoples settled next to the spring
and Jericho has been settled ever since. The beginning of civilization
was at hand in this area of the world. For hundreds of years various
groups of people came and went in the region. About 2000 B.C.E. a
nomadic Shepard from Mesopotamia by the name of Abraham
supposedly decided that there should be only "one omnipotent,
indivisible God". He essentially got the idea that God said if he
obeyed certain commands then he and his tribe would be given the
promised land of Israel. He thought that sounded pretty good so away
they went. Unfortunately years later "Mother Nature" got weird in
this area with drought. As a result his grandson Jacob took what was
left of the tribe and took off to Egypt. Food and work was available
there but within time they became slaves for 400 years. Fortunately
along came a guy named Moses and he snuck what was left of the
Israelites out of Egypt into the nasty Sinai Desert. This occurred
about 1,300 B.C.E. and they supposedly stayed in the desert for 40
years. During this time period the 10 Commandments were formed
and they really got their faith stuff together. This group of people
actually consisted of 12 tribes and they finally ended up going back to
the "Promised Land". During the next 200 years the 12 tribes
splintered away from each other with 10 going north and 2 going
south. They became craftsman and farmers. They appointed a king
named Saul. They founded a number of moral attitudes towards life
such as doing right, showing mercy, punishing evil, and doing justice
to those who are innocent. They were very humanistic in their

thoughts. King David was next in line and Jerusalem became the capital. Next came King Solomon who had made a huge temple. This was pretty neat but literally quite taxing to the populations. When Solomon died in 930 B.C.E. the 10 northern tribes went into revolt and formed a new capital called Samaria. All of this lasted for a while but in 721 B.C.E. the northern tribes were taken over by the Assyrians and actually became quite scattered all over the place. Then Nebuchadnezzar came in 586 B.C.E. and beat up the 2 southern tribes and packed them off to Babylonia. They even destroyed the temple and basically Jerusalem to show who was the boss. Fortunately for the Jewish people as they were now called 60 years later the Babylonians were defeated by the Persians. The Persians are today's Iranians. This is a very ancient civilization to say the least. Now to continue in 539 B.C.E. the Jewish people were allowed to return to Israel. They were still actually ruled by the Persian Empire. They soon busied themselves by building the Second Temple. Life went on for them. In 331 B.C.E. Alexander the Great defeated Persia and laid claim to Israel. Life went on for them. Then in 63 B.C.E. the Roman Pompey conquered Jerusalem and life went on although under Roman rule. Things went well if you yielded to Rome but in 66 C.E. the Jews had had enough of Rome and war broke out. The Jews lost, the temple was burned and thousands became slaves. Most likely about 100,000 died and another 100,000 became slaves. However, in 135 C.E. they somehow got it together and formed another revolt. They really lost this time and the Romans destroyed Jerusalem, outlawed the religion, killed the elders, and the Romans renamed the area Palestine. Many Jews escaped however and became true nomads all over the Middle East. Many Jewish slaves were also sent all over the Roman world. They may have lost Israel for now but not their Jewish religion. Then came the Middle Ages and here comes the crusades. Jerusalem must be saved from the dreaded Muslims. But these Christians also thought any Jews were "killers of Christ" so when they encountered any Jews it was not good for these people. They fled to north and east Europe to now modern countries such as Germany, Poland, Lithuania, and Russia. They also made it to Spain where they ultimately were told to convert or die. Over the years in

Europe they experienced good and bad times. An interesting point is
that they were somewhat stifled in what occupations they could do.
They were allowed however to become moneychangers and they were
quite adept in this occupation. Unfortunately during the 1930's Adolf
Hitler held them in very low esteem and of course the result was the
death of at least 6 million of them during the world's worst
experience. However good will somewhat prevailed since in 1948
surviving Jews founded the Independent State of Israel. They made it
back to the Holy Land but it was not an easy task. When the British
left Palestine the Muslin Arabs thought the land was there's for the
taking. The Jewish people had another plan since the land had been
allocated to them by the United Nations. They would of course
defend their territory. Soon Egypt, Syria, Transjordan, Lebanon, and
Iraq invaded Israel. Assam Pasha, Secretary-General of the Arab
League actually declared: "There will be a war of extermination and a
momentous massacre which will be spoken of like the Mongolian
Massacres and the Crusades". This was not to be as the Jewish
people carried the day. But this was not the end of it all. By June 4,
1967, 465,000 Arab troops along with 2,800 tanks, and 800 tanks
surrounded Israel. Arabs generally do not like Jewish people.
Feeling a bit strained Israel attacked on June 5th with all of their
aircraft except for 12 planes rapidly destroying 300 Egyptian planes.
They then basically wiped out the aircraft from Jordan and Syria.
Israeli ground forces then defeated Jordanian ground forces and took
over the Old City of Jerusalem. Now the entire Holy City was in
Jewish hands since Arabs had controlled this area of the city for years.
To add to their ultimate victory the Jews fought and took over the
Sinai and the Golan Heights, which helped to further protect Israeli
territory. They tripled the size of the area that they controlled from
8,000 – 26,000 square miles. Victory came but along with it came
750,000 Palestinian Arabs who were in the newly acquired territories.
Currently Israel does exist. They even have about 100 nuclear
weapons for big-time protection. The Palestinians are mostly to be
found in the areas known as the Gaza Strip and the West Bank. As a
general statement the Arabs still want to destroy Israel and go back to
Jerusalem. The Jewish people believe this is their rightful home and

will defend it to the end. A funny thing is that new studies have shown that if we took DNA from a typical Jew and a typical Palestinian Muslim there is a strong resemblance. In fact, the Y chromosome, which is what we study, is essentially the same. Both religious groups say they descended from Abraham. So it goes.

GENETICS AND GOD

About 95% of Americans believe in God and 70% feel there exists life after death. Faith is an interesting concept especially when looked at by a scientist. Scientists study what does exist and faith is essentially a concept of hope. Most humans throughout the world certainly hope that our life is not just a short experience on earth. That would be pretty silly but true faith has little in the way of scientific rationale. Sure it would be pretty weird if this is all there is to the whole show. I wonder if other organic species on other planets feel the same. Scientists have an idea that there are over 150 billion galaxies in the universe. Evidence is also showing that a galaxy may contain up to or more than 150 billion stars. That's a lot of stars in the long run and it is known that other stars have planets surrounding them. As of today we have been able to identify at least 340 extra solar planets. In 2005 scientists discovered the planet known as HD 189733b and what is unique is that the atmosphere contains water. It is actually a very large gas type planet like Jupiter but it has an atmospheric temperature of around 700°C. Now that is really hot so the water in the atmosphere can never reach the surface of the planet. What is kind of neat is that its star has such a great gravitational attraction on it that one hemisphere of the planet always faces the star. As a result only one side of the planet contains the water. Oh well it would not be a good one to live on but it shows that most likely other rocky planets do contain water. Water of course is needed for life on earth and probably for other organisms out there that are probably based on carbon. They may be based on silicon, which is closely related to carbon but silicon to silicon bonds are different being more loosely bound together. This would actually make these organisms much bigger than the organisms found on earth. Anyway faith is something we hope is true and that is sort of like thinking other beings exist in the universe. It will be difficult to scientifically deduce if so-called aliens exist. Its not like we can just travel out there and check it out. For example the closest star system to us is the Alpha Centauri System. It actually consists of 3 stars, which are 4.35 light years away from us. They possibly may contain life-sustaining planets. I wonder how long it would take us to get there? Well currently we travel in space about 35,000 mph. That's pretty fast but it's a slow boat in space travel time. Actually if we were able to go the speed of light (670 million mph) it would still take 4.35 years for us to get to this comparably close sun system. There goes big-time space travel for the foreseeable future! So for now we probably should place most of our hope and faith down here on earth. Actually one may want to ask why some individuals seem more inclined to really get into the concept of faith? Is it possible that a biological reason may be part of the scenario? Well what is going on right now is studies dealing with monoamines in the brain. They are the brain chemicals (neurotransmitters), which flow throughout the brain activating all kinds of areas involved with such things as mood and consciousness. One neurotransmitter is dopamine which is the feel good chemical. Another is serotonin, which can be involved, in negative emotions. We have found that a human gene exists known as VMAT2, which is involved in producing a protein that helps to package and transport these neurotransmitters. Scientists know that at least 2 variants of this gene exist and one of the variants seems to produce proteins better able to do the job correctly and efficiently. In other words if you inherit the good variant your brain chemicals flow better and you yourself feel better about yourself. They are even studying these genes to show the good genes help to inflect upon you a higher form of self-transcendence. Self-transcendence in a way can be defined as having the capacity to reach out beyond us to see the world as part of one great totality. This can deal with spirituality whereby one becomes aware that a higher source other than ourselves exists. So in a way the basic idea here is that those with the good genes are more likely to feel optimistic about life itself and therefore may be more inclined to believe in God. Now this is a pretty big assumption but it may have some merit. The concept of being religious certainly may have a biological component. But what we are taught as we grow up certainly is extremely important. Being raised in families that preach a certain religious doctrine basically helps to hard-wire the brain into thinking that religion is the true one. The individuals that believe in bizarre religions of the world can readily show this. These extreme religions, which will be discussed later, make the average individual just question how anyone could think they are the true way through life. Yet try to tell the person who has been totally indoctrinated into them that they are illogical to the extreme.

ONE HIGHLY INTELLIGENT GUY

As previously stated we became modern humans around 200,000 years ago. Slowly the population increased although there were some nasty times we almost did not make it. By 1804 the population of humans running around the earth finally reached 1 billion individuals. Now it is already past 6.5 billion and growing. That is a topic in itself and probably not a good one for the earth. Certainly throughout time some very interesting people were around and that is indeed the case for Thomas Jefferson. He was born on April 13, 1743 in a simple, farmhouse at the edge of the Virginia wilderness. Book after book has been written about him. He was a scholar, lawyer, scientist, gardener and architect. He of course wrote the Declaration of Independence and was a big-time President of the United States. He told Lewis and Clark to take off to the Pacific. He was an extreme reader of many subject areas. He was an obsessive letter writer leaving behind 28,000 letters of one sort or the other. He founded the University of Virginia. Thomas Jefferson wrote a very interesting book called "Notes On the State of Virginia" which basically discussed what was happening in this area at the end of the eighteenth century. He also discussed in the book such things as politics, science, religion, and even his thoughts on slavery. It is good reading. Jefferson had his own ideas concerning religion. As a confirmed deist he believed in natural religion and morality. He is said to have believed that mysteries beyond our human understanding should be set aside so that the mind would then be free to attack the real obstacles to happiness in life. Einstein with his brilliance also sort of thought of religion in those ways. Jefferson actually also believed in a supreme being who had set the world on its foundation and then stepped aside. He studied Hebrew and the Koran and tolerated all religions. He once said: "It does me no injury for my neighbor to say there are twenty gods, or no god. It neither picks my pocket nor breaks my leg". He led a life of morality and loved his fellow man. Still though he was thought by many to be against religion. To prove otherwise he seriously studied the Gospels of the Bible actually marking the passages that he thought represented the simple beliefs of Jesus. He ignored the others which he thought were just corruptions. He then wrote a 2-page summary titled "Syllabus of an Estimate of the Doctrines of Jesus Compared with Those of Others". Still then not done he wrote a 46-page booklet mostly for his family and friends titled "The Life and Morals of Jesus". Upon sending a copy to his friend John Adams he stated to him; " there will be found remaining the most sublime and benevolent code of morals which has ever been offered by man. I have performed this operation for my own use, by cutting verse by verse out of the printed book and by arranging the matter which is evidently his, and which is as easily distinguishable as diamonds in a dunghill". Jefferson was indeed a thinker! He also in general enjoyed his life as the President and actually followed a pretty neat schedule. On a typical day he would get up at 5 am and do paperwork until 9. He would then receive visitors. He would then have a cabinet meeting or would write letters until 1 pm. Then off he would ride on his horse around Washington. At 3:30 pm he would have dinner by himself. However 3 times per week he would host a dinner party for 12 invited guests. In full dress they would have 8 different kinds of excellent French wines and a large assortment of foods. A typical dinner may have included "rice, soup, round of beef, turkey, mutton, ham, loin of veal, cutlets of mutton, fried eggs, fried beef, a pie called macaroni, which appeared to be a rich brown crust … a great variety of fruit, plenty of good wines and good," according to the Federalist Senator Cutler. The dinner also included beer, porter, or cider. He then gave after-dinner talks until 6 pm. After this was over he would retire to write or to lose himself in thought. He of course was big into wines. In fact while at the White House he had purchased 20,000 bottles of European wine. Now perhaps his controversial arena was his apparent relationship with one of his slaves. Thomas Jefferson was born at a time when slavery was indeed big in the Colonies. However not all of the indentured humans were from Africa. According to Ben Franklin indentured servants who did most of the labor done in the middle colonies came from Britain, Iceland, and Germany. These individuals had to work for 5 – 7 years to pay off ship's passage. It is possible that between one-half and two-thirds of all immigrants coming to America at that time were involved in this scenario. Of course these people potentially could gain their freedom. It was much more difficult for the slaves from Africa. Even though this was the so-called period of Enlightenment the mental mindset of the times was that Slavery was not all that bad. Jefferson inherited an estate of 5,300 acres and later bought an additional 4,847 acres. He also had 35 slaves. When his father in law died he and his wife inherited an additional 11,000 acres along with 135 slaves. He ultimately kept about 80 slaves. He was actually somewhat opposed to this practice since in 1736 he appealed to the English Parliament "To put an end to this unchristian traffick of making merchandise of our fellow creators". The Parliament however was not to be swayed by the request. One of the slave families was the Hemmings that came to Monticello when Thomas wife's father died. This man, John Wayles had as his concubine Elizabeth (Betty) Hemmings who was part African and part European in ethnicity. Betty bore 6 children to John Wayles. One of the offspring coming to Monticello was Sally Hemmings who was only an infant at that time. Now the initial interesting thing about Sally is that she was the half-sister of Thomas Jefferson's wife Martha Wayles Jefferson. Martha was a true love of Jefferson but unfortunately she died in 1782 at the age of 33. She had given him 5 children. There names were Patsy, Polly, Jane, Lucy, and an unnamed son who only lived 3 weeks. Jane died at 18 months and Lucy only lived for 2 years. Only Patsy survived to old age and her younger sister Polly died at 24. Two years after his wife's death Jefferson traveled to France to be the American minister to France. He took along his daughter Patsy. Upon the death of Lucy Jefferson, he had his daughter Polly sail to France in 1787. He asked for a lady servant named Isabel to travel with Polly. Because she was about to give birth 14-year-old Sally Hemmings took the big ocean trip along with Polly. Sally stayed with them as a servant until their return to America in 1789. Shortly afterwards Sally had a baby who did not survive. Sally then stayed at Monticello as a seamstress and was responsible for Jefferson's room and wardrobe. Of course the plot soon thickened as Sally had other kids while at Monticello. Harriet was born in 1795 but only lived 2 years. Then a son named Beverly was born in 1798. A daughter who did not survive infancy was then born. Then the daughter also named Harriet was born in 1801. Two sons Madison and Eston were born respectively in 1805 and 1808. A funny thing about all of them was that they all closely resembled the features of Thomas Jefferson and could pass as white people. Another interesting thing was that Tom was present in Monticello at the time all of them were conceived. So of course it became somewhat of a controversy that this famous man could father children to his possible concubine. Could Tom have been totally enchanted with Sally? After all she was the half-sister of his departed wife and was very fair in complexion and probably physically resembled his wife. Well of course the controversy has gone on for a couple hundreds of years but now we have DNA evidence to show it most likely was indeed true. As many humans are well aware human females contain 2 X sexual chromosomes and males an X and a Y chromosome. The Y chromosome is rather small and undergoes few genetic mutations over time. In 1998 Dr. Eugene Foster of the University of Virginia obtained Y-chromosomes from 5 descendents of Jefferson's paternal uncle, Field Jefferson. Tom himself had no son lineage from his first wife. Field's DNA would work out to perfection in the world of genetics. He also obtained Y chromosomes from a descendent of Eston Hemmings. By studying the haplogroup areas of the Y DNA, which contain common markers the matches were found to be perfect. The Hemmings at least in the case of Eston are direct descendents of this famous man. But that is not the end to it all. Currently the National Geographic Society is sponsoring the Genographic Project, which is studying the DNA of individuals throughout the world. They recently approached another descendent of Jefferson known as Odine Jefferson. His DNA was again that of

Toms and to further the interest they have now checked where that DNA may have originated. Thomas having red hair would be thought to be Irish or Northern European. What they found was that the certain genetic markers now being investigated show that his Y chromosome actually originated somewhere in the Middle East. It is possible that Jefferson's main male ancestor came to England from the Middle East perhaps as a merchant somewhere around 3,000 years ago. We are getting real good at understanding where we came from but in the long run we still have Mr. Jefferson's Y chromosome floating around in American society which is great. Now to finish up with Jefferson he had a huge estate needing lots of work and care. Unfortunately even though they were well cared for his slaves did much of the overall work. He had a real big garden to keep going. He designed his garden to be 668 feet long and 80 feet wide. He initially set out almonds, apricots, and 198 cherry trees of different kinds from Italy. He even tried planting 1,500 olives stones. He tried to grow rice and grapes. He loved planting apple trees of which Spitzenburg was his favorite. He grew 300 different kinds of vegetables, including 40 types of beans, 2 dozen kinds of English peas, and 17 different kinds of lettuces. He was one of the first to bring to America Brussel sprouts, eggplant, cauliflower, and broccoli. He also messed with tomatoes, which the Europeans thought were somewhat poisonous. What is most interesting is that he knew the concept of refurbishing the garden with nutrients that had been depleted over time. He actually undertook tests to determine exactly how many cattle would be needed to revitalize a given area of soil. He added cover crops like clover and vetch in the fall to be dug into the soil in the spring. He even understood that native ground cover applied around the garden would limit erosion. As he once stated in 1785: "Cultivators of the earth are the most valuable citizens. They are the most vigorous, the most independent, the most virtuous, and they are tied to their country wedded to it's liberty and interests by the most lasting bonds". Thomas Jefferson led a most interesting life of 84 years. Unfortunately for him he periodically suffered from horrible migraines of which little medicine was available during this time period.

THE MISSING METABOLITE

What may potentially happen to your automobile if you consistently only have one half of the amount of lubricating oil in it. Well the car will still most likely work but the engine will deteriorate at a faster pace. It may also not last as long churning up hundreds of thousands of miles. Such is the way for the human body. We all know we need certain nutrients in optimal amounts to stay healthy. These of course include the minerals and vitamins and fortunately modern nutrition is teaching us about the optimal levels needed. Unfortunately one of the vitamins is still not considered by many to be needed in the amounts necessary for good health. The vitamin is ascorbic acid commonly known as vitamin C. All animals for a number of very specific reasons need it. As a result almost all of the members of the animal kingdom synthesize it in their bodies from simple glucose sugar. A few animals somehow experienced genetic mutations millions of years ago, which caused them not to be able to synthesize vitamin C from glucose. These include a few fish and insects. It also includes the indian fruit bat and a bird known as the red-vented bulbul. Luckily these two characters eat huge amounts of vitamin C enriched fruits. The guinea pig can also not synthesize vitamin C. A funny thing is that it is known to suffer from many human related illnesses. As far as primates go an unknown biological mutational event occurred about 25 million years ago to an ancestral primate. The making of vitamin C in primates is due to a four-step enzymatic process and this mutation caused primates not to be able to make one of the essential enzymes. As a result all of today's living primates cannot synthesize their own vitamin C. For most of them this is not a cause for concern since they consume a high plant based diet high in vitamin C. Unfortunately for humans our diet could never provide an optimal amount. It has been estimated that a 150-pound animal roughly synthesizes up to 5,000 mgs of vitamin C per day. It should be quite logical that if an animal makes large amounts of this vitamin C then it utilizes all of it on a daily basis. Vitamin C is not stored to any extent in an animal's body. This vitamin has many functions of which the most important is maintaining healthy collagen levels. Collagen is a major protein, which is our connective tissue. In humans along with other mammals collagen is basically the cement or glue that holds all of our tissues together. It allows our organs to contain many different types of tissues and maintains our blood vessels. To show how important collagen is just think about scurvy for a minute. For hundreds of year's sailors developed scurvy while spending long times at sea. They were not getting enough vitamin C and their bodies just sort of fell apart. More will be said about the specifics at a later time. Anyway thousands upon thousands of men died because of a lack of vitamin C containing foods. All they needed was a paltry 7 – 10 mgs per day of this vitamin to avoid the disease that slowly caused their body to fall apart. Vitamin C keeps the collagen intact by donating an electron to an iron atom. The enzyme propyl-4-hydroxylase is needed to keep collagen healthy and have a proper structure. Iron needs to be attached to it for it to be active and the iron atom has to have a proper charge. Typically iron is found in our body in the ferric (Fe^{+3}) state. This enzyme in order to be activated must have the iron in the ferrous (Fe^{+2}) state. When vitamin C donates an electron to the ferric iron it changes into the ferrous active state. It is pretty wild that our body can fall apart due to a lack of vitamin C being available to add a silly electron to an iron atom. But that is the way the body works in this situation. Now one may ask what else the human body does with vitamin C. Well here is a short list.

1. It is secreted into our stomach at the rate of approximately 60 mgs per day where it functions to neutralize poisons.
2. It maintains and protects the heads of sperm from damage from poisons.
3. It activates many enzymes through electron donation, which produce many of our cellular hormones.
4. It helps to open up our blood vessels by causing artery-lining blood cells to produce prostacyclins.
5. It increases the good cholesterol HDLs.
6. It helps to regulate our body's cholesterol levels by activating liver enzymes that regulate bile cholesterol levels.
7. Through electron donation it has been shown to inactivate toxic metals.

8. Through electron donation it also rejuvenates vitamin E that has been busy neutralizing poisons in our body.

9. Vitamin C helps to boost our overall immune system in a number of ways. It increases the production of interferons, which help our cells recognize viral attacks. It also causes our white blood cells to produce more skeletal proteins so that they may move faster to the sight of an infection.

10. It aids in iron absorption from the intestines into the bloodstream.

11. It lowers the risk of developing cataracts by neutralizing poisonous superoxide free radicals in the eye.

12. It can be concentrated in white blood cells where it functions to neutralize many of the free radicals generated in the process of destroying bacterial and viral germs.

This is actually a rather short list since vitamin C is involved in many other cellular reactions involving electron donations. But by far and away a most major job of this vitamin is to neutralize the countless poisons taken into the human body on a daily basis. The word poison is to a biochemist a rather general term. Much of the poisonous substances we encounter are actually called free radicals. In an easy to understand definition a free radical is a highly unstable substance, which is in dire need of an electron. So what they do when they get into our body is rip electrons from our cellular parts. This includes our cell membrane, organelles, and even our DNA. In other words they damage us slowly but surely over time. Examples of free radical poisons would include benzene from car exhaust and the huge amounts of tars found in cigarettes. Chlorinated substances from our drinking water also become free radicals in the body. Charred meat from cooking grills adds radicals to our body. Our cells even generate superoxide free radicals from a biological mishap that occurs in our energy making mitochondria in our cells. Actually we now live in a world full of chemicals, which get into our body through food, air, and the water we breathe. They are a major factor in our aging and disease processes since they slowly but surely damage the body over time. Fortunately we have a wonderfully complex series of enzymatic reactions in our cells which function to neutralize most of the free radicals. They do this mostly by very simply donating an electron to the free radical, which makes it stable and harmless to the body. But we indeed are being overwhelmed with the onslaught of these radicals from our industrialized world and we need all the help we can get. Here is where vitamin C comes into play. This vitamin is the best water-soluble antioxidant there is and if it comes in contact with a radical it readily donates an electron to it. Neutralization has been accomplished. By consuming optimal levels of this vitamin we can ensure ourselves that the liquid parts of our body will contain large amounts of this most important vitamin. Now of course it is well known that if we take in a large amount of this vitamin at one time we will urinate out a somewhat substantial amount. Our kidneys do not have a great ability of sending this vitamin back into circulation in the bloodstream. That is ok for a couple of reasons. For one it is good to have vitamin C in the bladder, urethra, and ureters since it neutralizes poisons in the excretory system. It has also been found that slowly the kidneys will actually learn to increase its ability to recirculate vitamin C back into the bloodstream. So it is most certainly wise to start taking anywhere between 1,000 to 5,000 mgs per day of this most important substance for good health and to minimize the aging and disease processes.

MODERN MEDICINE

It takes a stupid person to not realize that modern medicine has been a great factor in how humans now enjoy a much better life. At least that is true for the more fortunate countries in the world. Unfortunately millions upon millions of us live in horrid conditions in many parts of the world. Still perhaps there is some hope for many of the unfortunates at least in some situations. Take for example Africa in which many areas for thousands of years have had to deal with a most horrible worm. It is known as the guinea worm (*Dracunculus mediinensis*) and it can grow up to 3 feet long with a width like a typical paper clip. Unfortunately millions of Africans live in villages where the only water source is a shallow unprotected well or even a stagnant pond. We might as well start with the well water to understand its life cycle. These wells or ponds are typically polluted with many nasty substances and creatures. A common organism is a small microscopic water flea known as cyclops. Cyclops tends to like to eat the minute embryos of the guinea worm. We will soon see that millions of these microscopic embryos get into the water supplies from the adult female guinea worm. The embryos instead of being digested by the cyclops water flea actually live and grow into larva in the body of this simple flea. Humans come around and drink the water, which contains the water flea and the larva then pass into the human intestine where they start to grow. Within a year they mature into long adults and mating occurs between the male and female worms. The males then die but the females break through the intestine wall and travel through the body. They cause intense burning pain rendering the victim unable to do much of anything but suffer. Then these long up to 3-foot long females go to the victim's skin and her tail region secretes an acidic substance allowing the tail to pass through the skin and actually stick out. In order to relieve the pain and suffering the unfortunate usually goes back to any available water and lies in it. Although the worm usually emerges from the feet and legs it can actually come out through the eyeballs and just about any other body region. Well as soon as the villager goes into the water this stimulates the adult female worm to expel 1-3 million embryos out of her genital pore and hence the cycle repeats itself. We estimated that in 1986, 3.5 million humans harbored these nasty worms. By 1995 the numbers had decreased to 130,000. Fortunately only 12,000 cases were recorded in 2006 and we are close to actually getting pretty much totally relieved of this menace. Now one may ask is it modern medicine that has found some great chemical, which can kill the embryos when they get into the intestinal tract? The answer is a big no! Actually no medicine is known to kill the embryos, larva, or the adults. The only way to remove the adults is by a method used for thousands of years. The tail sticking out of the skin is tied up with string and the adult is slowly wound around a stick just a little bit at a time. If one pulls too hard the worm snaps in half leading to a nasty infection. This winding of the adult worm around the stick may take up to 2 months before the entire worm is expelled. Slow but efficient I would guess. So what actually has been done to limit this worm on the human condition? Well, the answer is education and the major guy involved is the past President of the United States, Jimmy Carter. He and his wife have founded The Carter Center whose aim is to eliminate many of the diseases of the Third World. With the use of many helpers going into various villages in the world the people are taught about the worm and drinking clean water. If possible they are taught to boil their drinking water or to filter it through a nylon fine mesh filter, which captures the water fleas. They are taught to not put their infected parts into water for relief from the stinging sensations. Finally new clean wells are being dug and a pesticide called Abate to kill the embryos is added to wells and ponds. Hopefully within 5 years this scourge of humans will be gone. Now that hopefully is a good story with a positive ending without the imput of modern medicine. But we now live in a complicated world where many of us believe there is a pill for just about everything. Take cholesterol for example. So much bad information has been given to society stating the nastiness of this substance and why we need to really keep cholesterol levels low in the human body. What many do not realize is that cholesterol is a most necessary substance for our body and we really need certain amounts of it. Every cell in our body demands it as it is a necessary part of the cell membrane. It helps to maintain the shape and integrity of the membrane. Without it the cell would die. It is also needed to make vitamin D in our skin when sunlight shines on it. It is needed to make bile, which helps our intestines breakdown dietary fats. A most important role is that it is the essential component of our myelin sheath, which forms outside of most of our brain cells. This sheath helps to regulate the speed of electronic signals traveling across the brain cells. If it breaks down one develops multiple sclerosis, which can be a horrible disorder. The body has developed a wonderful mechanism for regulating our circulating cholesterol levels. Yet still it is common knowledge that over the years cholesterol may build up on the inner lining of our blood vessels. Over time this may narrow the artery enough so that one may experience a heart attack or stroke. So we are told to limit the amount of total cholesterol in the body in order to avert any of these 2 conditions. Well the theory may be somewhat correct but just limiting cholesterol levels does not necessarily lower any risk factor. It is much more complicated than that and that has been known by many scientists for years. The actual regulation of cholesterol levels occurs in our liver. Our liver has the capability of producing all of the cholesterol we need from glucose sugar. We actually do not have to eat animal products since they are our only source of dietary cholesterol. We should also be aware that we actually only have a very limited capability to actually send dietary cholesterol from the intestines into the bloodstream. Most of what we eat actually is passed out in our solid wastes. That is one reason why eating lots of cholesterol-rich eggs does not boost cholesterol in the body. Think about it for a second. All animal products contain cholesterol so if we eat animal stuff for breakfast, lunch, and supper we should be overloaded with the stuff. But we are not and even giving up animal products does not reduce levels all that much. Try not to tell that to a typical medical doctor though. Anyway it is the liver that monitors cholesterol levels. If the levels are low then the liver just makes more cholesterol to send into circulation. It should be a great monitoring system but due to genetics some individuals get a liver that does not monitor the levels as well as it should. As a result often too much is sent into circulation and this is why some peoples total cholesterol is too high. You can blame your parents on that one but still most people with somewhat high cholesterol levels do not have heart attacks or strokes. Actually many with low levels do have heart attacks or strokes. The real villains in this scenario are those dangerous free radicals circulating in the bloodstream. Yes I am talking about the stuff from cigarettes, car exhaust, and the water we drink. You see cholesterol is not water-soluble so it cannot just flow through the bloodstream and arrive at our cells. It has to hitch a ride on some water-soluble substance. That substance is known as a low-density lipoprotein (LDL) which many doctors call the bad cholesterol. That is bad terminology since cholesterol has to get to the cells. The LDLs are the structures, which carry it deep inside of their fatty-protein shell. So these LDLs are needed for transport. We should also note that unsaturated and monounsaturated fatty acids also get a free ride inside of the LDLs. They also have to make it to our cells and they also are not water-soluble. Well here is where the problem actually arises. As the LDLs are taking the cholesterol and fats to our cells they often encounter free radicals in the bloodstream. These nasty radicals then rip electrons from the LDL and if the damage is severe enough it becomes an oxidized damaged free radical. The body can no longer use it and so what happens is a white blood cell comes along and eats up the damaged LDL full of cholesterol. That's one of the jobs of our immune systems white blood cells. If this white blood cell picks up enough of these damaged LDLs it gets bigger and bigger in size. Now typically the white blood cell should move out of the bloodstream through minute openings in the arterial wall where it can then go and be destroyed by other body processes. But in easy to understand terms it is too big and gets stuck in the arterial opening where it basically dies. Due to complicated mechanisms the cholesterol then gets deposited and attached to so-called sticky areas on the inner arterial wall. So over a period of many years of free radical onslaughts loads of cholesterol may be deposited in the arteries. The inner walls narrow and over time get ragged. If blood platelets in the bloodstream hit a ragged area they may explode leading to a blood clot. The result may be a heart attack or a stroke due to a loss of oxygenated blood needed in the critical area. So free radicals play a highly significant role in heart attacks and strokes. To minimize the possibility of this situation we should take as many antioxidants (electron donors) as possible to neutralize the radicals. Of course a real good idea is to slow down the intake of free radicals. Vitamin C is great for the liquid areas of the bloodstream and vitamin E protects the fatty-rich exterior of the LDLs. Natural antioxidants found in fruits, vegetables, and even green tea also provide us with excellent sources of free radical fighters. Actually the more colorful the fruit or vegetable, the higher the amount of flavanoid antioxidants they contain. That is definitely the way to go and many doctors now know and advise the goodness of these foods. But they are a big part of the huge pharmaceutical industry and this industry likes pills. Actually some of the biggest selling drugs sold throughout the entire world are prescribed to actually reduce circulating cholesterol levels. For a number of years now the logic of the pharmaceutical companies has been that if we can slow down the production of cholesterol in the liver then we should have less plaque build-up. So they went about making a number of statin drugs such as Lipitor. This medicine functions to inhibit a most important enzyme known as HMG-CoA reductase. This enzyme converts a wild naming substance called 3-hydroxy-3-methylglutaryl-coenzyme A into a substance that will become cholesterol. If this enzyme is somewhat inhibited then less cholesterol is made in the liver. It is as simple as that. Lipitor also increases the ability of the liver to recognize how much cholesterol is in circulation. So as a result this causes less LDLs to be circulating in the bloodstream thereby lowing total LDL levels. To doctors this meant less potential for heart disease and strokes. Other medicines have also been made including Vytorin. Vytorin is kind of interesting since it also inhibits the enzyme HMG-CoA reductase so less cholesterol is made in the liver. But it also keeps some of our dietary cholesterol from making it from the intestines into the bloodstream. Both medicines sound pretty good but recent research is that they do not stop the build-up of plaque on the inner walls of the intestines. That is because it is the free radical damage to LDLs that causes the build-up as has already been explained. To make matters worse these medicines may have severe side effects. For one they may damage the liver in some people who take them. Another very bad potential problem is that they may cause severe muscle weakness known as

Rhabdomyolysis. The muscle weakness appears to occur because these drugs breakdown an important substance in the cells known as Co-Enzyme Q-10. This substance is very important since it helps to move energy-making molecules into the mitochondria of our cells. If Co-Enzyme Q-10 is destroyed energy cannot be made in the muscle cells and muscle fibers actually break down and are released into the bloodstream. To add insult to injury these broken down muscle fibers may travel to the kidneys actually damaging them. Of an interesting note this problem is well known in Britain and anyone taking these cholesterol-reducing medicines are prescribed Co-Enzyme Q-10 supplements. Now of course not everyone taking these medicines suffer these problems but it is common knowledge that the potential exists for problems. Many people know other people who suffer from taking these medicines so it must be more common than the pharmaceutical industry would like to admit. So some good advice may be to instead of going the modern medicine way just limit free radicals into the body and take in lots of antioxidants.

THE BIG BANG SINGULARITY

Without a doubt here is where the word theory most certainly is applicable. Hundreds upon hundreds of scientists have devoted huge amounts of kinetic energy trying to figure out how this darn universe came to be. The complete details are far from being totally refined but through intense studies and mathematical calculations here is somewhat the general idea. Much of this information is derived from the exceptional mathematician Steven Hawking and the noted physicist Brian Green. Give or take 13 billion years ago all of the potential energy of the universe was compressed to the size that makes the dot at the end of a typical sentence look enormous. It was known as a singularity. Something big to say the least happened and it is not considered to be an explosion. An expansion would be a better term and it was real hot at the initial time period. It has been estimated that prior to 10^{-47} seconds after the initial expansion, the temperature was 10 billion billion billion (10^{28}) degrees celcius. At this incredible early time period all of the forces and particles were considered to be one. It is also theorized that by 10^{-35} seconds that the inflationary expansion of the universe occurred by a factor of 10^{30}, 10^{50}, 10^{100}, or more. Please do the math on that one but anyway the universe got real big in a very short period of time. At around 10^{-43} seconds physicists believe a most extraordinary event occurred. This theoretical event if shown to be true may be one of the most amazing discoveries in all of science. Einstein and many others have attempted for years to understand basically the unification of all universal events. In other words what are the true simplified fundamental forces of nature. Well, it is theorized that at 10^{-43} seconds after the Big Bang that only one force existed in the universe but at that time period 4 new forces were starting to be produced. They were produced from changes that occurred in the one force. First the force of gravity was produced and this may have occurred as early as 10^{-43} seconds. Then shortly after 10^{-43} seconds when the temperature was below 10^{28} degrees celcius the strong nuclear force was produced. It separated away from the weak force and the electromagnetic force. So in an exceedingly brief period of time the 4 known elemental forces of the universe were produced. To put this into a better perspective the strong force is the one that holds the nucleus of atoms together. The weak force is responsible for radioactive decay. The electromagnetic force deals with the interactions between electrical charges and can be attractive or repulsive. Finally the well-known force of gravity is the attractive force between any 2 pieces of matter in the universe. Scientists have been busy trying to figure out the math and physics of how these 4 forces were once one and what was the composition of the initial one force. They know the components of 3 of the 4 forces but the composition of the force of gravity is not known. It is suspected that particles called gravitrons exist but they have not been found. It is the quest of many investigators to come up with the Grand Unified Theory which if found will show that all 4 forces were indeed one in the early universe. Albert Einstein spent much of his later years trying to put the whole scenario together but the force of gravity always stumped his incredible mind. Perhaps with the new Large Hadron Collider we may soon find the answer that eluded Einstein and many others. But now let us continue with the story. Shortly after 10^{-35} quarks began to be produced, and by 10^{-10} the quarks had formed their way into protons and neutrons. Within 3 minutes after the Big Bang it is theorized that the universe was a nearly uniform gas of about 75% hydrogen and 23% helium with a very small amount of lithium elements. Now when we say uniform that only includes the elemental matter of the universe. Actually only 5% of our universe contains visible matter such as the protons, neutrons, and electrons that make up the elements found in the universe. So what makes up the other 95%? Perhaps one may think it is just void or empty space. That would be the wrong answer. Edwin Hubble once again showed that the universe is expanding and that could only happen if matter and energy is involved. To put this in a better prospective let's take a look at what Stephen Hawking in his wildly acclaimed book "The Universe in a Nutshell" states: "Various cosmological observations strongly suggest that there should be much more matter in the galaxy and other galaxies than we see. The most convincing of these observations is that stars on the out-skirts of spiral galaxies like our own Milky Way orbit far too fast to be held in their orbits by the gravitational attraction of all the stars that we observe. We have known since the 1970s that there is a discrepancy between the observed rotational velocities of stars in the outer regions of spiral galaxies and the orbit velocities that one would expect according to Newton's laws from the distribution of the visible stars in the galaxy. This discrepancy indicates that there should be much more matter in the outer parts of the spiral galaxies". Physicists believe that the discrepancy is due to a type of dark matter that is believed to make up 25% of the universe. Nobody knows what it actually consists of. Dr Hawking surmises it may be very light elementary particles such as axons or neutrinos. He further offers the possibility that it could be WIMPs –"weakly interactive massive particles". WIMPs have been predicted to exist by scientists but have not been observed. Perhaps this is where once again the 7 billion dollar Large Hadron

Collider will be useful. But finally to top out this entire universe stuff is where is the other 70% of matter, which is still out there? Again nobody knows but mathematical evaluations state it must exist for the universe to be expanding at the rate it is. A funny thing is that Albert Einstein actually in the early 1900's thought that the universe was actually static and not expanding. This bothered him a bunch since his mathematics showed that gravity alone could not keep a static universe. He believed he would have to dink around a bit and add a repulsive force to keep the universe from not expanding. He called it the cosmological constant and mathematically it showed perfectly a static universe. But when Hubble showed the universe was expanding Einstein called it his "greatest blunder". That is actually too bad because Einstein actually thought that his General Theory of Relativity should propose that the universe actually was expanding. But he did not trust his original equations on the matter. If he would have we would not call the Big Bang by that name but would call it Einstein's Bang. But anyway we now think that his cosmological constant was justified in a way since the dark matter of the universe has replaced the constant. He was very close to perfection on that one. So from a final thought we will probably soon find dark matter but if not there will have to be a big revision of the Big Bang Theory.

FUNCTIONAL FOODS

We certainly live in a modern world that contains a big population. The quest for feeding the population is going to continue to be a most pressing demand for many years to come. Scientists and others are busily investigating all kinds of options one of which is genetic transfer. Here is a rather interesting example. Many different kinds of edible plants are damaged by the various caterpillars of moths, and even a few butterflies. For example, ripe corn is often damaged by the European corn borer, and cabbage crops by the harmful cabbage butterfly. A great organic way of stopping the damage is to apply a certain type of bacteria to the crop before it is getting ready for harvest. *Bacillus thurengensis* (Bt) is a very specific bacteria that kills caterpillars.

If a caterpillar is eating a plant that has Bt on it the bacteria goes into the digestive system. A toxic protein is then produced by the bacteria, breaking open the gut of the caterpillar. Spores from the bacteria then go out into the body of the caterpillar and it dies a poisonous death. Bt is harmless to humans and other forms of wildlife. So here is what has been done. Scientists removed the gene from Bt that codes for the making of the poisonous protein. They have added it to the DNA of such crops as corn and cotton. Now when these crops grow they actually produce in their tissue the toxin. When caterpillars eat these plants they also eat the poison and that does in the caterpillars. We do not have to spray these crops with the bacteria. Now that is some pretty neat genetic engineering. To take this scenario a step further lets look at a pretty bad problem not typically known by most humans. It is estimated that over 1 million children die worldwide due to a vitamin A deficiency. Furthermore about 3,500,000 children go blind every year due to a lack of vitamin A. This condition is called xerophthalmia and the lack of vitamin A causes the cornea of the eye to ulcerate and become highly inflamed. This results in the blindness. It is estimated that 140 – 250 million pre-school age children are at risk for this horrible problem. These kids tend to live in the poverty stricken countries of the world and for many a major food source is rice. They get very little of the vitamin A rich foods such as liver and dark-green leafy vegetables. It is possible though that soon help will be on the way. Beta-carotene found in carrots and dark-green leafy vegetables is an excellent source of vitamin A. In fact beta-carotene is actually 2 vitamin A molecules bonded together. When we consume beta-carotene the bond is broken and we end up with 2 vitamin A molecules to use for the body. Of course we actually take in millions of beta-carotene molecules from these foods. What is really neat is that scientists have now taken out the genes for making beta-carotenes from daffodils and dandelions and have added them to the DNA of certain strains of rice. It is called golden rice and even some of the beta-carotenes can be found in the starchy areas of the rice. This is a new functional food and in theory golden rice could be a lifesaver for millions. Just eat the rice and get vitamin A. It sounds great but is just now getting off the ground but hopefully the world will come to the rescue of these millions of kids before it is too late. Unfortunately only time will tell since producing, marketing, and delivery of this form of rice is not happening at a fast enough pace. Now functional foods do not just involve gene splicing. One can actually just add certain substances to a food source in order for it to be a functional food. Take chicken eggs for an example. Eggs are a great source of nutrition for an easy to understand way. A chicken egg when fertilized will become a chick in 21 days. A rooster fertilizes the hen through a method known as the "cloaca kiss". The hens store the sperm and produces eggs from her ovaries. When she lays an egg her fertilized zygote is now found in the big egg. That is unless it is a small bantam chicken then it would be found in a little egg. Anyway as it well known the hen keeps the eggs warm and allows nature to do its stuff. All of the nutrients needed for a baby chick to be produced must be in the eggs. This includes complete proteins, carbohydrates, fatty acids, minerals, and vitamins. Now chicken cells require the same nutrients as humans cells so for humans the egg is the perfect food. Sure it contains lots of cholesterol since all animal cells need it but that is good. Research has confirmed that the consumption of eggs does not really raise cholesterol levels in humans. That is pretty much a myth. For once again humans do not absorb large amounts of dietary cholesterol in the first place. Secondly eggs contain large amounts of lecithin (phosphatidylcholine), which is needed for the cell membrane of all animal cells. It is also an important brain chemical. What is really nice about this lecithin substance is that it inhibits the ability of cholesterol from leaving the intestines and entering the body's circulation. This is a major reason why egg consumption does not increase the bloodstreams cholesterol level. So eggs are great and perhaps they can even be made better. Let's make them into so-called "Designer Eggs" and really boost their benefits. In a small laying flock it is easy to add both vitamin E and selenium to their foods. Selenium as will be shown is a great reducer of free radical damage lessening cancer risks. Vitamin E is a great fat-soluble antioxidant. We can give the birds lots of green plant material allowing the eggs to be full of beta-carotenes. Eggs are also natural sources of the related compounds lutein and zeaxanthin, which are great antioxidants for the retina of the eye. We can add flax oil to their feed and then the eggs will be full of alpha-linolenic acid. Humans cannot synthesize this fatty acid and few foods contain it. It is necessary since it inhibits inflammation in the body and boosts the immune system. It also reduces blood clotting in the bloodstream thereby reducing the risks of heart attack and strokes. We can also throw oily cold-water ocean fish to the chickens. Blue fish and mackerel are cheap excellent examples of big-time oily fish. They really are cheap if you catch them yourself. So what is up with the oil? Well, these fish and other cold-water ocean species are loaded with oil that is high in docosahexanoic acid (DHA). This is the major omega-3-fatty acid found in cold-water ocean fish. It is hardly found at all in warm-water ocean fish and fresh-water species. DHA is the major fatty acid found in the human brain. That is why fish is called brain food but the catch is only the cold-water species. DHA has many other positives. It reduces cholesterol levels and decreases blood pressure. It inhibits the incidence of blood clotting and reduces the risk of stroke. It increases the good HDL cholesterol. DHA helps to increase calcium levels in the bones. It raises dopamine and serotonin levels in the brain. It may even reduce the symptoms of inflammatory bone disease. Finally DHA may reduce the risk of developing colon, breast, and prostate cancer. All of that sounds pretty darn good to me! But that is not all to this adventure. Two of the best nutritional foodstuffs on the planet are the members of the *Allium* and *Brassica* families. The first family makes up the onions and garlic type foods and the second family is the cabbage bunch. Their members include broccoli, mustards, collards, kale, and some exotic Asian vegetables. Both groups are loaded with all kinds of nutrients and phytochemicals. In the case of the *Alliums* it is the sulfur containing phytochemicals that are great for the body. Garlic for example contains a host of sulfur derived allicin (S-allyl-1-cysteine) chemicals. When the garlic is crushed the allicin further decomposes into a whole slew of different bioactive phytochemicals. These phytochemicals function to inactivate various poisons and help to get them out of the body by way of the bloodstream. Garlic is also great in that it can reduce blood pressure, thin the blood, act as an antioxidant, and even lower cholesterol levels a tad. What is of extreme interest to medicine is that selenium is an element that has many similar chemical properties to sulfur. It actually is in the same group with sulfur on the periodic table of the elements. Research has now found that if we grow garlic and onions in soil that is enriched with selenium then these plants will take up the selenium. After much of the selenium moves up the roots it is added to the allicin chemicals replacing the sulfur. That's nice but so what? Well specific studies have shown that allicin containing selenium instead of sulfur is at least 300 times more powerful as an antioxidant and more powerful in reducing cancer risks. Consuming these selenium-enriched substances will also add unique organic selenium substances to our diet, which are wonderful antioxidants. The *Brassicas* are also a unique group of vegetables in which the major phytoactive chemicals also contain sulfur. This phytochemicals are also very anticarcinogenic in nature. They are known as glucosinolates and upon chopping or cutting up these vegetables they breakdown into a number of highly active compounds. These sulfur-containing compounds are also good at inactivating bodily poisons and ushering them out of the body. Once again if we grow any or all of the *Brassicas* in soil that is loaded with selenium many new selenium-derived glucosinolates will be produced. These compounds as is the case with the *Alliums* are much more powerful in reducing the risks of developing cancer. I am sure in years to come that we will develop many more functional foods, which can only be a positive for human populations.

WHY POSSIBLY GAY AND HAPPY

We now know of over 1,500 animals that have exhibited homosexual actions. The small flatworm (*Pseudobiceros hancockanus*) even gets into penis fencing. Male lions often have sexual encounters with other male lions even though this is to ensure loyalty. Orangutans have been observed making and using dildos made of wood and bark. Some scientists are really studying this stuff! For example we know about 8% of male rams prefer to have sex with other rams instead of the ewes and it is not due to dominance. Could this possibly have a biological explanation? Well a major structure in the brain of mammals is the hypothalamus. This area has many functions including pleasure and reward systems such as eating, drinking, and sexual activities. Of interest is that in sheep the hypothalamus contains an area known as the ovine sexually dimorphic nucleus. It deals with sexual activities. Studies in the rams that like rams have shown this area is different in rams and ewes. It is much bigger in the rams who like ewes but is much smaller in the rams that like rams. Its size is more like the typical size in ewes. This certainly does not prove why a ram likes other rams but it should be noted that good evidence is coming out that homosexuality is very much regulated by our biology. We will attempt to address the biological basis as is currently being examined in humans. It should first be noted that there probably is not a "gay gene" as has been investigated. Our genetics of course is quite complicated and most likely multiple genes and environmental aspects play a big role. However in sticking with chromosomes and genes certain markers have been found in homosexuals. Females are interesting in that they contain 2 X sexual chromosomes but in each of their cells 1 of them is inactivated. It does not work and it is haphazard in each of the women's billions of cells which one gets inactivated. It is entropy at work. An intriguing study of women who have gay sons and women who have straight sons came up with a really strange find. In a highly significant number of the women who had gay sons they had a specific inactivation of the same X chromosome throughout their cells. That is really strange and highly unusual from a biological perspective. Very few of the mothers who had straight sons had this situation and their chromosome inactivations were random, as nature has intended it. It is possible that the mothers having the specific inactivations carry an assortment of genes on that chromosome that influences homosexual tendencies. Of added interest is some of these women who have a number of gay sons was found that specific gene sequences on chromosomes 7, 8, and 10 were shared by 60% of the gay brothers. The region on chromosome 10 correlated with homosexuality only if that specific chromosome came from their mother. Now other biological situations have also been found between homosexual men and heterosexual men. For example once again the hypothalamus is an incredibly important area in the brain stimulating or inhibiting many human functions. One of these is highly involved with sexual activities. An area of the hypothalamus known as INAH3 is located in the medial preoptic area and is specifically involved with sexual expression. Studies of heterosexual men and homosexual men have shown that this area is much larger in heterosexual men. In homosexual men it is much smaller as is also true of females. Another area known as the sexually dimorphic nucleus is also located in the preoptic area. This area is about 2.5 times larger in males than in females and contains roughly 2.2 times more cells. Studies in homosexual men have shown that this area is significantly smaller than in heterosexual men. Furthermore the suprachiasmatic nucleus of homosexual men has been found to be 1.7 times bigger in homosexual men than in heterosexual men and females. It also contains roughly 2.1 times as many cells. Although mainly functioning in circadian rhythms it is being investigated in regards to sexual orientation. Now a specific question may be why differences exist in these areas of the hypothalamus. It is indeed possible that a mixture of unknown genes may have an influence on the development of the hypothalamus. However a possible big influence may possibly be due to hormones produced by the pregnant women and the fetus during gestation. It is well known that testosterone-like androgens cause a fetus' brain to develop into male dominating male patterns. Likewise an absence of certain androgens leads to the female brain pattern. This of course is mostly regulated by whether the fetus is XX or XY as far as sexual chromosomes occur. However the pregnant women also supplies differing levels of androgens and also female estrogens to the fetal environment. It is at this time hypothetical but quite possible that a relative absence of androgens during critical brain development may lead a male to actually ultimately possess a somewhat feminized brain leading to changes in hypothalamus development. A high level of androgens during female fetal development may also partially explain female homosexuality. These hormonal amounts could possibly explain other brain connections still not adequately evaluated. For example we know through MRI and PET scans heterosexual males and homosexual females have a rightward asymmetrical symmetry. On the other hand, the cerebral hemispheres of homosexual males and heterosexual females were found to be symmetrical. Much more research is needed to quantify these findings. However we do know that the brains of these different individuals do indeed exert differing patterns to certain stimuli. We are aware that males produce a testosterone-derived chemical in their sweat glands. We also know that females produce an estrogen related chemical, which has been isolated in urine. It has been documented that homosexual males respond to the male testosterone substance just like heterosexual females. The heterosexual males responded to the estrogen chemical. Of biological interest is that olfactory signals sent their message to the medial preoptic area of the hypothalamus in both homosexual males and in females. Furthermore male sweat has been shown to cause the hypothalamus of females to release luteinic hormones that can stimulate possible ovulation. Estrogen production is involved in this process. We should note that estrogen injections in homosexual men cause them to also release luteinic hormones. Estrogen injections in heterosexual men fail to elicit this response. Finally we are aware that homosexual men and heterosexual men respond differently when given antidepressant SSRI medications. SSRI medications keep serotonin levels at higher levels in the brain and hypothalamic serotonin is involved in sexual arousal and expression in males. After taking the SSRI medications homosexual men had significant less glucose metabolism in this area of the brain than in heterosexual men. This is just another example of the different brain chemistry of these 2 types of individuals. So from a final perspective much more needs to be learned about homosexuality but it most certainly has a biological basis without even investigating environmental perspectives.

WE ALMOST LOST THESE TWO

Two of the most famous cities of the world are of course London and Paris. Both are rich in history and the central parts of each contain magnificent structures. Huge crowds flock at all times of the year to breathe in the rich history and see the architecture. They were almost lost to us during World War II due to the madman Adolf Hitler. As is well known Hitler basically wanted control over the world and started the invasion of Europe on September 1, 1939 by invading Poland. Within time France was occupied as well as the Low Countries such as Belgium and Holland. A large German Army occupied Paris by June 20, 1940. Then it became time to hopefully slow down Britain. Hitler actually had funny feelings about this country and in a way hoped they might not be a true enemy. For him the real enemy was Russia. Unfortunately for him Britain had Sir Winston Churchill and appeasement to Hitler was not in his thought patterns. Not having even close to an adequate invasion plan Hitler could only strike England from the air. War between the 2 started in many places but it was the air battles known as the Battle of Britain, which helped save the islands. Ultimately stymied by the British Air Force and not able to amount an invasion his demented thoughts turned to Mother Russia. A vast war machine and Air Force invaded Russia on June 22, 1941. The beginning of the end one might say for Germany. But for now I need to get back to December 29, 1940. Things were not well for Britain. The United States was certainly not yet in the war.

Britain did have the British Fleet but their war-making industry was far from being anywhere near that of Germany. However, Churchill during September sent a squad of 40 bombers to bomb Berlin as a sign that they would not quit. Even though it did little damage an outraged Hitler decided to start bombing the cities of Britain. He did throughout the fall inflicting much damage but the bombing of the City of London during the evening of December 29th was a biggie. The City of London actually deals with London's old "square mile". It stretches from the western end of Fleet Street eastward to the Tower of London, and north from the river Thames to the London Wall. This area was in use by the Romans by the first century C.E. and was called Londinium. The great Saxon king Alfred the Great made it the capital of his kingdom. Through the Middle Ages it swelled in buildings along with the population. It was almost totally destroyed by the "Great Fire of London" in September of 1666. In fact over 13,000 houses and 400 streets were reduced to ashes. The job of rebuilding went to the famous mathematician and architect Sir Christopher Wren. He rebuilt 87 parish churches and other buildings such as the Guildhall, which is the center of city government. His major task was to rebuild his masterpiece, St Paul's Cathedral that was finished by 1710. The massive cathedral is the seat of the Bishop of London and Wren had installed a massive lead-sheathed dome. It rises 365 feet to the cross at its summit. It also has an organ with 7,189 pipes and 108 stops. It is famous to say the least. Adolf Hitler certainly wished for its destruction. The actual day of the raid coincided with the fact that the position of the moon would cause abnormally low tides on the Thames River Valley. The Thames around the City of London would then only be a narrow stream with little water available for putting out fires. The muddy banks would also prevent fire fighters from even getting to the water. It was also on a weekend and much of the population was away and buildings were locked up making it hard for fire fighters to enter. So on that night the commanding general of Luftflotte 3, Generalfeldmarshal Hugo Sperrle sent planes out of fields near Paris to the City of

London. One plane type was the Heinkel He 111s medium bomber. It could carry a bomb load of 4,400 pounds. The load could consist of 8,550-pound bombs or 8 canisters of incendiaries. The other type of plane was the newer Junkers Ju 88A. This plane could hold a 6,400-pound payload. Using the relatively new "X-Apparatus" helped finding the City of London in darkness. The pilots had at their disposal a radio receiver that picked up a high-frequency radio direction beam. The beam was being transmitted from a station along the coast of Normandy and it was being aimed directly towards the City of London. Just follow the beam and it could even tell you when you were 10 minutes away from the target. The first wave of aircraft for the attack consisted of 135 – 145 planes and they dropped mostly incendiaries. Soon to follow was the second wave that was somewhat bigger in numbers and dropped 550-pound high-explosive bombs. Buildings all over the City rapidly caught on fire. Over 1,500 combustions from the incendiaries were documented. Fires burned out of control all around St Paul's Cathedral. The Cathedral was hit but survived the onslaught. Entire warehouses and the communication network were wiped out. The fires could not be controlled mainly because of a lack of water. The low tide on the Thames did its job quite well. Roughly one and one-half miles of the City was laid to waste and the City was brightly lit from all the fires. The German planes during the night made it back to their bases near Paris and were they in for a surprise. The German chain of command had authorized that these pilots load up with more bombs and go back and do it again. Strained and tired to say the least they prepared once again for the journey to Britain. But Mother Nature had other plans for them. It rained and rained and rained at the German airfields. The runways soon became totally choked with mud. Taking off was near impossible and so Feldmarshal Sperrle had no choice but to postpone the second raid. The rain and clouds continued for days and the second raid was finally cancelled. The Germans really did not know the amount of horrendous damage they had dealt the City. If they had the chance to send out the second raid the City of London would have been totaled. The fires in the City lit up the sky for miles and the planes would have had an easy time blasting the target area. St Paul's Cathedral would have been finished along with just about every other building in the area. The City of London would no longer exist. Mother Nature saved the day and the City was able to rebuild. Another famous city almost lost it during the war. Paris of course has a rich history. The area around the city has been inhabited for at least 6,000 years. Julius Caesar conquered the Celtic Parisii tribe there in 52 B.C.E. It was named Lutetia and renamed Paris in 212 C.E. It grew over the years and by the 12th century started to show its architecture. The Cathedral of Notre Dame de Paris was started to be built in 1163. The initial construction ended in 1345. It of course was the center of government and religious life. The world famous Louve museum was first started to be built in the 16th century. Currently housing about 35,000 works including the Mona Lisa it is one of the most visited museums in the world. The famous Pont Neuf Bridge was opened for traffic in 1607. Napoleon commissioned the Arc de Triomphe to be built in 1806 to commemorate his military victories. The Eiffel Tower, which rises 984 feet tall, was built in 1889. Many more fabulous buildings are to be found in the city. Adolf Hitler invaded France on May 10, 1940 and the German army swept into Paris only 40 days later. Paris stayed under German occupation for 4 more years. On August 9, 1944 Hitler appointed Generalleutnant Dietrich von Cholitz as the military governor of Paris. He was partly chosen since he was "an officer who had never questioned an order no matter how harsh it was". He had led the whole German blitzkrieg in the west in 1940. He was also the first German officer to invade the Low Countries. He even commanded the bombers that wiped out Rotterdam before it could surrender. He even ordered the execution of the Jews in Russia. He was a real nice Nazi! In Paris he had a 20,000 man garrison and lots of nasty things happened to people who were caught in the underground. During this time period things were not going well for Germany. General Dwight D. Eisenhower had 37 divisions racing through France towards Germany. He very well could have liberated Paris but at a high cost to the city itself. He decided to bypass the city partly due to this concern but also he did not want to slow down his armor. He worried that a prolonged fight there would dry up the gasoline, which was a critical need at the time. He also knew that he had to get 75,000 tons of food and medical supplies towards the German border for winter storage needs. While the Allies were at work Cholitz was busy working diligently in the city. However in many ways Adolf Hitler by now was a ruined man. He ordered Cholitz to keep fighting in Paris to the last man. He also issued an order to him to reduce the city to a pile of ruins if all was lost. Cholitz did his job real well as 1 ton of explosives were placed in the Chamber of Deputies. Furthermore 2 tons of explosives were put in the basement of the Invalides and 3 tons in the Crypt of Notre-Dame. Most of the other major buildings such as the Arc de Triomphe and the Eiffel Tower were to be destroyed. By mid August 1944 the Allies were closing in on Paris. Members of the 4th U.S Army Division and the 2nd French Army Division were soon to enter Paris. Hitler tried to send 2 SS divisions to the city along with tanks. He also ordered a massive bombing by Luftflotte 3 on the city. He even wanted as many V1 and V2s as possible to blast the city. On August 25, 1944 the liberation of the city began and fighting ensued. It was time for Cholitz to order the destruction of the city. But a funny thing happened and Generalleutnant Cholitz had a change of heart. He knew destroying the city would only gain a few days of time for Germany and the world would never forgive that country if Paris were gone. Even though Hitler wanted to know "is Paris burning" he could not go through with the plan. It was cancelled and the city survived. He waited seated at a long table to surrender and when Lieutenant Henri Karcher of the army of General de Gaulle entered the room it was all over. He was released from Allied captivity in 1947 and died in 1966. A man who oversaw horrible things thought through his brain and allowed Paris to survive. So it goes.

WAS HITLER A DESCENDANT OF THE NEANDERTHALS

The first real Neanderthal skeleton was found in a quarry in 1856. The quarry was located in the Neader Valley east of Dusseldorf, Germany. Hence the name was given Neanderthal man. Scientifically it is now called *Homo neanderthalensis*. Within time the skeletons found showed many unique differences to modern man. They were very robust and heaviness of build. Their body was very squat, compact, and they had short powerful limbs which were somewhat bowed. Their shins were very short in proportion to their thighs. The head was most unusual with long and low skulls with a sort of bun-shape at the back. The brow arches were bigger than anything found in modern humans and they had a huge nose. They were made for living in cold conditions. The males average about 5 feet 5 inches in height and the females 5 feet 2 inches. The largest specimen was found at Amud, Israel and was about 5 feet 8 inches tall. It had a brain size of 1774 cc's. In fact the average brain size of Neanderthals was about 1600 cc's in males and 1300 cc's in females. That is larger than modern human brains but these individuals really were not brain smart. Through some minor genetic mutations pre-Neanderthals probably branched off from *Homo erectus* in Africa between about 400,000 and 650,000 years ago. The complete separation occurred around 376,000 years ago. These years are somewhat argumentative as a 2007 study utilizing DNA showed a divergence of 800,000 years ago. Anyway small groups slowly moved out of Africa as early as 350,000 years ago and moved to the Middle East, Western Asia, and Europe. By 150,000 years ago they showed all of the characteristics of the true Neanderthal and they were definitely settled in Europe. It appears they were gone from Western Asia by 50,000 years ago. During most of their existence in Europe the weather was cold. They tended to live in small groups by caves and really kind of stayed put. They hunted and scavenged for their foods. They made use of fire and made somewhat crude stone tools. They had lots of animals to eat. Things like mammoths, reindeer, musk ox, rodents, birds, bisons, and even the big aurochs were plentiful. Our modern cattle are direct descendents of the now extinct aurochs. One may wonder if they had the ability to speak? Well they did possess the same type of hyoid bone as found in modern humans. It connects the muscles of the tongue to the larynx, which allows for speech type movements. Their hypoglossal canal, which carries the hypoglossal nerve, was actually bigger than found in modern humans. This nerve controls the muscles of the tongue. DNA shows they possessed the same FOXP2 gene as found in modern humans that again is involved with speech and language. I doubt though that they had a gifted vocabulary though. It appears they just sort of lived from day to day. They did not store their food for example. They did not seem to have heavily defined family relationships. They did though bury their dead on occasion sometimes even in the fetal position. However no real religious or spiritual type ideas are evident from their burials. Of interest is that their skeletal remains show lots of nutritional problems, which should be expected. A heavy meat diet, which at times may actually have been sparse, would lead to deficiencies of many vitamins and minerals. Their skeletal remains show fractures, arthritis, dental problems, and even signs of infections. But somehow they were pretty successful as they made it for thousands of years in the nasty European climate. But then around 45,000 years ago modern humans started to pop up in Europe with their higher intelligence. They had to come upon each other from time to time but slowly they were only found in small pockets. By 30,000 years ago they were pretty much gone although some groups survived for a while in Spain. What happened to them is conjecture. Is it possible they bred into the modern human line or did the smarter modern humans drive them to extinction? Nobody has a great handle on what exactly happened. We do know that between 99.5% of the DNA between the both groups is the same. It certainly is possible some casual mating occurred which would have been fun to watch from a primitive standpoint. We may soon find out the answer to this question. The Max Planck Institute for Evolutionary Anthropology and 454 Life Sciences have acquired the nuclear

DNA from a Neanderthal and are working on sequencing it. We may shortly know the answer as to whether interbreeding occurred. But for now it is hard to say if Hitler had Neanderthal blood. We have none of his DNA and his body was partially burned after he did himself in. Most likely his remains where taken by the Russians and buried somewhere in Russia.

THE COW

Lots of people like the cow, (*Bos Taurus*). They are fun to eat to many of mankind and their milk can be used for drinking or making into cheese and yogurt. It is also interesting as to how they developed from the nasty auroch, (*Bos primigenius*). This ox-like creature evolved inn India about 2,000,000 years ago and made it to Europe 250,000 years ago. It became extinct in Poland in 1627 C.E. It could reach 6 feet 5 inches tall at the shoulders and weigh 2,200 pounds. It possessed lyre-shaped horns set at a forward angle and liked to kill early humans. Julius Caesar stated this about them in *Gallic War* Chapter 6.28;" those animals which are called uri. These are a little below the elephant in size, and of the appearance, color, and shape of a bull. Their strength and speed are extraordinary; they spare neither man nor wild beast which they have espised." They certainly sounded quite nasty but about 8,000 years ago tough humans living in Southern Caucasus and Northern Mesopotamia started the long process of domesticating them and changing their gene pool. This process also occurred in Northern Africa and India. Many years later the domestic cow was produced and of course many varieties of it exist today. They are pretty docile characters but watch out for the bulls. A nice book on cows could be produced but this segment is involved with some new health-associated characteristics of their meat and milk. The milk is of major interest here and especially a fatty acid found in milk. It is known as conjugated linoleic acid (CLA) and probably 99% of the world's population has never heard of it. We certainly know that a certain amount of fat is found in cow's milk. It is also found in the lean fat of the cow. Typically the common holstein produces 3.62% fat in her milk. So 2% milk contains roughly one-half the amount of normal fat found in milk. Skim milk of course has had all of the fat removed, which is actually a shame since milk fat is easily digested and burned as energy. It mostly consists of short-chained fatty acids, which we can readily burn as an energy source. The conjugated linoleic acid fatty acids are also removed in making skim milk. Anyway what is up with conjugated linoleic acid (CLA)? It actually is very unique since it is only produced by ruminants. These are the mammals with a bunch of stomachs and their stomachs are loaded with billions of bacteria. The actual job of these bacteria is to take the grasses and grains that the cow digests and break them down into nutrients and billions upon billions of new bacterial cells. These excess bacterial cells are then ultimately broken down into the proteins and fatty acids that actually cause the cow to grow and get bigger. Its weird biochemistry but cows actually grow mostly from the digestion of bacterial cells. Of course carbohydrates, vitamins, and minerals are also made from the breakdown of the grasses and grains. Anyway CLA just happens to be one of the types of fatty acids produced by these unusual bacteria. In fact cows that are mostly allowed to graze on pastures produce far and away the most conjugated CLA. Typical grain fed cows do not produce nearly as much as those that can roam around and enjoy the scenery. The grass fed cows produce up to 7 times the amount of this fat than the grain girls. New scientific information is showing this type of unusual fatty acid has many potential health promoting properties. Of interest it has been shown that this fat may reduce the risk of developing a number of cancers. The actual mechanisms are still being investigated but it appears CLA may help keep cancer cells from developing or actually help to destroy them. CLA intake may also help to bolster our immune system through a number of mechanisms. It may also help to slow down the progress of plaque developing on our arteries and may reduce hypertension. It may help in regulating our body's ability to utilize glucose. CLA has also been found to potentially help people to lose weight by stimulating energy aiding genes in our adipose tissue. This certainly sounds like an interesting fatty acid so what is the best way to get it into our body? We can take supplements of it but right now evidence is suggesting that is not the best method. Instead consume milk products or eat lots of cheese. Cheese is actually a really good concentrated food source and it can contain lots of CLA. Cheese is also high in protein, calcium, good fats, minerals, and fat-soluble vitamins. It is also low in lactose, which is good for lactose intolerant individuals. The lactose is broken down in the cheese making process. Cheese making of course is an art where originally milk was stored in sacks made from sheep and goat stomachs. Unbeknownst to these nomadic herdsman wild lactic acid bacteria landed on the milk fermenting the lactose into lactic acid. An enzyme in the stomach called rennet allowed the milk to turn into cheese curd. Ultimately the watery whey was drained out and what was produced was a bland cheese. Having a low pH it did not readily spoil and a new foodstuff was formed. Of course today it is much more complicated but still lactic acid bacteria are the initial bacteria in cheese making. Rennet, albeit from a vegetable source still makes the curds and the whey is ultimately separated. To make the different cheeses various types of bacteria and or molds are added throughout the process especially the aging process. The cheeses containing the highest amounts of CLA come from grass fed cows with the highest levels from the alpines of Europe. The softer cheeses tend to have more CLA than the aged cheeses. So feel free to eat cheese with perhaps some wine and get some good conjugated linoleic acids in your diet.

EINSTEIN'S BRAIN

Most of the kids who go through schooling learn about Albert Einstein. He was of course the genius mathematician and physicist of the early 20th century. He sort of figured out how the universe works. That says a lot in itself. More will be written about him later in this text. But for now lets just look at a couple of interesting things about him. He got deep into relativity, which is that the fundamental laws of physics are the same, whatever your state of motion. We humans on earth are certainly in motion. A person at rest is actually spinning with the earth's rotation at

1,040 miles per hour. To top that out the earth is also orbiting around the sun at 67,000 miles per hour. That may be interesting but Einstein had other ideas up his mind. In 1905 he published his "Special Theory of Relativity" which can be explained nicely by Walter Issacson. In 2007 he published a great biography on Einstein even though he is not a scientist. To him this theory shows," that measurement of time, including duration and simultaneity, can be relative, depending on the motion of the observer. So can the measurements of space, such as distance and length. But there is a union of the two, which we call space-time, and that remains invariant in all inertial frames. Likewise, there are things such as the speed of light that remains invariant". That is well put about this theory. However a few years later Einstein was bothered about this theory. It only worked with uniform constant-velocity motion and not with changing speed or direction. It also left out gravity in the overall equation. So he went deep into his visual mind for the next 8 years trying to improve the theory. In 1916 he published his "General Theory of Relativity". He basically said that matter causes space to curve and that gravity is actually a curved field and not a force. This curved field is in the space-time continuum that is actually created by the presence of mass. Sounds good to me! Anyway none of us live forever on this planet and Albert Einstein died in 1955 at the age of 76. He succumbed to a ruptured aneurysm of the abdominal aorta. A Quaker named Thomas Harvey rapidly did a routine autopsy. Einstein was cremated in Trenton, New Jersey and 12 people attended his funeral. His ashes were sent into the Delaware River. He did not want a grave as he thought people would come to it with a morbid fascination. However, not all bodily parts were cremated. During the autopsy Harvey decided to remove his brain. He hoped to keep it a secret but told his family. The next day at a local elementary school a teacher asked the class what was new in the news. A young girl said that Albert Einstein has died. Then a young boy spoke up and said, "My dad's got his brain". Well the news reached Einstein's family and they figured out it may be good for science and so did not make a

stink about it. They also sort of forgot about it. Harvey had a
pretty good idea of what he was doing. The whole brain was
fixed in a 10% formalin solution and externally studied. The
cerebral hemisphere was then cut into about 240 blocks, each
about 10 cm^3. They were then embedded in celloidin and various
histological cuts were made. Celloidin is a sulfated and nitrated
form of cellulose, which can be used in a solution. It is very long
lasting as a preservative at room temperature. It also hardens into
something resembling plastic. Dr. Harvey placed the brain parts
in mason jars and kept them in a red plastic picnic cooler. The
jars for some reason were labeled "costa cider". He kept the
cooler in his office of all things. Twenty years later a writer for
"Harpers" magazine took Dr. Harvey and the cooler to California
to visit Einstein's granddaughter. Evelyn Einstein wanted to have
his DNA tested but they found that the DNA had become
denatured and useless. However all was not lost on Einstein's
brain. Researchers in the 1980's were working on the average
glial/neuron ratio in certain parts of the human brain. Neurons of
course are the typical brain nerve cells from which chemical
messages pass through the brain. Glial cells, which are more
numerous than neurons, surround the neurons and have a number
of jobs. They help to maintain the neuronal circuits and in some
cases make the myelin sheath. They help to repair myelin. They
help to keep the neurons from infections and toxic wastes. They
also provide a large amount of the nutritional needs of the
neurons. In fact they divide and increase in number with more
active neurons. Dr. Marian C. Diamond in the 1980's was a
neuroanatomist at the University of California, Berkeley. She was
busy studying glial/neuron ratios from certain areas of the human
brain. She found out about Einstein's brain and 3 years later was
sent 4 sugar cube-sized pieces from his brain. Through a detailed
investigation of normal male brains and Albert's they found that
in all 4 areas he had many more glial cells per neuron than the
others. In the left inferior parietal region this was most
pronounced. Of interest is that this area of the brain analyzes or
associates inputs from other brain areas. This is an area of

"higher" mental function and having more glial cells may have allowed this area to work on "super-charge". That certainly is neat to an anatomist and in 1999 in the journal Lancet another look at his brain was researched. Dr. Sandra F. Witelson at the McMaster University in Hamilton, Ontario got his brain stuff and analyzed it against a number of normal male brains. In examining his parietal lobes it was found that this area was 15% wider than in the other brains. They also showed that the sylvian fissure was located in a unique area. Its location may have possibly allowed neurons in this area to communicate more easily. The additional width of the parietal areas is extremely interesting as this area is involved with mathematics and spatial thinking in terms of space and movement. So what does this mean in the long run? Well one thought is that Albert Einstein inherited certain genetic patterns that allowed for the development of the brain as it did in his case. But would that brain area develop as it did if he had nobody pushing him mentally. Most likely not as our environment plays a big part in how our brain develops. Fortunately he had a good upbringing with caring parents who wanted him to get a good education. He had a good early start contrary to public opinion and went deep into the studies of math and physics at an early age. The rest is history!

MORMONISM

Two identical twins shortly after being born are adopted. A religious Jewish family adopts one of them. A religious Mormon family adopts the other baby. Life is good for both and they are raised in the doctrine of each specific religion. They grow up and suddenly meet each other for the first time. They ask each other which is the right religion and most likely they profess that the one they studied was the real one. Of course this is only natural as we do inherit the genes we do but our environment plays a huge role in our behaviors. Such is so often the case with religion. When we grow up deeply in a specified religion it is only natural to presume that this is the truest of the true. Our brain does become somewhat hard-wired into that specific religion. That is quite obvious from some of the really hard to understand religions of the world that are just too far fetched to be real. Of course educating oneself through deep studies may change ones look on things. And of course educating oneself through deep studies may tell you that perhaps you were right in the first place. Religion as has already been discussed involves hope and faith. There is no science to it and proving it to be true just isn't going to happen. There certainly are many religions to choose from. Take the Jehovah's Witness as an example. Charles Taze Russell believed Jesus came to earth invisible in 1874 and he prepared for Armageddon to come in 1914 C.E. He founded the religion and people were baptized and they studied their own translations of the Bible. They do not believe in Christmas, blood transfusions, symbols of nationhood, or voting. They also reject military service and saluting the flag. It is their role in the world to go out and tell people the end time is coming and that only 144,000 from all of earth's people qualify for heaven. That is too bad since there currently are over 5 million Jehovah's Witnesses. Good luck to all of them. By the way Charles Taze Russell died in 1916 and his last wish was to be buried in a toga! Now Mormonism is also somewhat of a different religion. Joseph Smith Jr. who was born in Vermont in 1805 to a very religious Christian family and founded the Mormon religion. At a young age he became torn between Baptist and Methodist preachers. In the spring of 1820 while taking a walk in the woods he had a vision of light, terror, and darkness. He says he saw in his vision 2 people who were pointing to each other. He heard a voice stating, " This is my beloved son, hear him". Joseph asked the 2 people which sect he should follow? Then he made a big decision. He decided then and there that all Christian sects had it wrong! So he went on a mental quest for a few years trying to figure things out as such. In the fall of 1823 as he was busy praying for forgiveness he was awed by the bright lighting of his cabin. A white figure appeared and said he was Moroni, the son of the prophet Mormon. He stated that God had a special mission for Joe. He would soon be shown a book containing the "Fullness of the Everlasting Gospel" as told by Jesus to the ancient inhabitants of America. This group was a lost tribe from the Old Testament that had somehow made it from the Middle East to America thousands of years ago. Joseph was also told that the Book of Mormon was written on golden plates and he was to prepare himself for Christ's return. The golden plates were hidden under a hill 3 miles from his farm. He went there and upon lifting stones and touching the plates an angel showed up and said it is not time to understand the plates yet. Of interest is that nobody else can be proven to have seen the plates but 3 individuals professed to have seen them. Part of the writings from the plates stated that Hebrews came to ancient America where the nasty sinful Laminites had wiped out the virtuous and industrial Nephites. Smith added to this scenario that Jesus came to America after the resurrection thereby giving Christian roots to this nasty place. Other parts of the book are also of interest. For example persons of the Trinity were actually people. Ancestors of those of Mormon faith may be baptized and saved. Human souls have preexisted. You will inherit the afterlife as a god. The 10 tribes of Israel will be restored. Well, things got rolling for Smith after the book was published in 1830. He recruited members from New England and moved to Kirtland, Ohio and built a temple. Twelve apostles were chosen along with priests, bishops, and a president. Within time they moved to Kerr, Missouri along with 15,000 members. They were not well received and riots ensued with many deaths of the membership. So they packed up to Nauvoo, Illinois. The president of the 12 Apostles, Brigham Young was then sent to England to draw people to American and this new religion. Thousands of mostly poor people came over and before you knew it Smith decided he wanted to be emperor and practice polygamy. He declared himself a candidate for the Presidency of the United States. The political situation in Illinois soon got nasty and armed gangs began to threaten the Mormons. The Illinois governor tried to settle the mobs by telling them charges would be filed against Joseph Smith Jr. They included fraud, power lust, and polygamy. Smith then went to Carthage, Illinois and stayed in a visitor's cell in the jail pending trial. However 200 men assaulted the jail and Smith tried to flee but was shot dead. Over 25,000 attended his funeral and his body was secretly buried. Ultimately Brigham Young took the flock to the Great Salt Lake and for a while the times were very difficult. But the gold rush came about and as the caravans passed by the lake the Mormons started to prosper. But they were still big into polygamy and President Zachary Taylor did not go for that. He refused to allow this area to become the state of Utah. But then he died and Brigham Young said, " Zachary Taylor is dead and gone to hell, and I am glad of it". That is a nice religious statement to make. Well soon Utah became a state and Young was appointed Governor in 1850. The religion prospered even getting some Indians to join since they were ancient ancestors. Young had about 47 kids and 20 or so wives. But polygamy was embarrassing the United States Congress and in 1857 President James Buchanan ordered troops to go to Utah and restore order. So the Mormons got together a 2,000 legion force and tried to get help from the local Indians. But the Indians had other plans as they were going to wipe out a caravan of immigrants going westward with 350 head of cattle. They told Young that they wanted the Mormons to help them and if not they would join the U.S force. So Young decided to help but in a deceitful way. When the caravan showed up the Mormons led the assault but fired over the heads of the immigrants. But the Indians not to be outdone slaughtered all 120 men, women, and children. President Buchanan was kind of furious about that and sent 1,500 troops to Salt Lake City but winter closed in on them. By spring peace came about and Albert Cumming as governor replaced Young. The Civil War descended upon the States and President Abraham Lincoln had little time for Utah. He stated, "Tell Brigham Young that if he will let me alone I will let him alone". Within time polygamy was abolished and a major building effort has made Salt Lake City the big city of Mormons. They are currently going throughout the entire world spreading the message and today are one of the world's most rapidly growing religions. Of an interesting sidelight it is possible that Joseph Smith Jr. and perhaps other religion originators suffered from Temporal Lobe

Epilepsy. Of course this is only conjecture but theoretically possible. Temporal Lobe Epilepsy (TLE) consists of a number of disorders where there is abnormal electrical stimulation arising from one or both temporal lobes of the brain. It is still not known exactly what the cause of this disorder originates. However, it is known that newborn babies may develop an infection resulting in a fever. They have at this time in their life an immature thermoregulation system and in some cases the temperature may go too high for too long. This can cause febrile convulsions that sometimes may last for an hour. This may alter brain chemistry in the future leading to TLE. Even a head injury may be the cause and although modern medicine works well today that was not so in years past. Perhaps something like that happened early to Joseph Smith Jr. A very common type of TLE is known as Simple Partial Seizures (SPS). People having SPS events tend to stay conscious but experience all kinds of sensations. They may experience euphoria or fear. They may feel they are floating, flying, or even leaving their body. They have religious and mystical experiences. They very often see visions and hear visions. Studies on them have shown that during an SPS event they often respond emotionally to religious words. Now once again we probably will never know if the visions encountered by Joseph Smith Jr. were due to TLE but most scientists feel those having these episodes most likely have an unusual brain event.

SEX

Mammals of course have sex mainly to continue the species. Alligators and snakes also have sex, as do most of the reptiles. Birds once again utilize the cloaca kiss. Humans get into the thing in their own messy ways. But when we really get into the whole concept it is *Pan paniscus* that takes it to a totally new level. Most humans have never even heard of the pigmy chimpanzee. The real name for it is the bonobo. It was not even discovered until 1929. These chimpanzees only live in one isolated area of the world. They are only found in the Democratic Republic of the Congo in the tropical lowland rainforest south of the Zaire River. Nobody really knows how many still exist. Some say 50,000 exist and other put the figure all the way down to 5,000. Most likely the number is closer to the 5,000 mark. They have been hunted for food (bush meat) and loggers and miners have destroyed much of their habitat. Some of the local population likes to utilize their bones since they say they are a good potion for pregnant woman. Of course this is horrible but fortunately the United States has founded the Bonobo Conservation Initiative. With cooperation with the shaky Congolese government 11,803 square miles of rainforest has been established as a Bonobo reserve-type park. Hopefully with cooperation with the locals their numbers will increase. Unfortunately they do not have babies until 11 years old or so and then may have them at 5-year intervals until menopause. But that sure does stop them from having sex since typically the whole group has casual sex everyday of the year. They are total sex fiends to say the least. Most people when they think of chimpanzees think about *Pan troglodytes*. That is the common chimpanzee found in zoos, movies, etc. This species lives in a variety of African habitats ranging from humid forests to dry savannah woodlands. Although there may exist 200,000 wild chimps the populations are being seriously threatened. Millions of them existed 100 years ago but logging, hunting, farming, and loss of habitat is really taking its toll on the species. Hopefully the world will wake up to the devastation of wildlife and even ocean fish before it is far too late. The chimps are of course our closest biological relatives. We share up to 99% of the same DNA even though the common chimp sort of has the mentality of a 4 year old in many ways. But they actually are pretty darn smart. For example, they travel around a lot and they remember when certain crops are ripe. They hold grudges, nurse resentments, and even harbor thoughts of revenge. Sounds kind of humanistic in many ways. They also even grieve over the death of kindred and can recognize themselves in a mirror. I guess that makes sense since of the 4 billion base pairs in the DNA of humans and the common chimpanzee there are only 160,000 pairs that differ. But they also have their nasty side. They can get really mean and have even been known to kill little kids in Africa. Some authorities believe they mistake the kids for one of their favorite foods the Western Red Colobus monkey. They are really strong as their upper body strength is roughly 5 times that of humans. Males can be downright nasty to other males. In fact one male may recruit other males to help him fight another male. Males from different tribes may fight to the death. But it is not always bad since males tend to groom each other and after a fight the 2 males may hug. Male chimps are often pretty nasty with the females and are known to eat their babies. Females on the other hand are more submissive yet females do not form strong bonds with each other. They tend to mate when they are 10 years old or so. They actually have a type of menstrual cycle of 34-35 days in length. She is only receptive to the male for 7 or 8 days of the cycle. They give birth at close to 9 months and the kid hangs around closely for about 5 years. When their kid reaches adolescence they break away from their mother   All in all if pretty much left alone they have a pretty good life of 40 years or so. The oldest chimp in captivity is now 78 and was in some Tarzan movies. Now lets get back to the bonobos. They split off from the common chimp about 1 million years ago. They are really different than their cousins. They are smaller in size and tend to walk upright more of the time than the common chimp. They tend to stride with their shoulders squared and they do not slouch as much. They actually look like an *Australopithecus* humanoid. Once again they live in the rainforest where food is plentiful. They mostly consume fruits but also eat small invertebrates. Having a plentiful food source is one reason these animals are extremely mellow in nature. They are not aggressive in nature and are actually highly sensitive. In fact during the bombing of Hellabrun, Germany during World War II all of the bonobos in the zoo died of fright. The common chimps were not fazed by the noise. The bonobos have a very interesting social life. The females are the dominating influence in the tribe that may number up to 100 individuals. This may sound like a lot but they tend to forage in groups of like 8 -10. The males are very submissive to the females especially the more alpha types. Their main joy in life other than eating is having casual sex. This includes males with females, females with females, and even males with males. In this scenario we are not talking about homosexuality since pretty much anything goes. The only taboo is that a mother will not have sex with her son once he reaches adolescence. That is good for the gene pool. Another interesting gene pool thought is that often an adolescent female will leave her group and travel to and settle with another group miles away. So what goes on sexually with the bonobos is a sex researchers dream come true. At any time during the day a male will casually bond with a female for an intimate contact. The average length of the sexual encounter is 13 seconds with an average of 45 penile thrusts. Of interest is that often these encounters are face to face which was once thought to be only found in humans. This position may occur since the females penetration area is positioned much further forward than in the common chimp. These male and female bonobos after having this short encounter will often have sex many more times during the day with other members of the clan. Female bonobos also have a menstrual cycle of 35 days but they are sexually receptive almost all of the time. Even after giving birth they become sexually active within a year whereas the common chimp takes 3-6 years to get back in the game. Females also enjoy activities with other females. Most commonly what occurs is called genito-genital rubbing (GG rubbing). What happens here is that 2 adult females will come together and face each other. One female facing the other clings with arms and legs to the partner. She then lifts her off of the ground and they rub their genital areas together whole emitting grins and squeals. Males can get real crazy. In times of stress one male will spread his legs and present his penis to his adversary in a friendly gesture. To top this off, they also like to do "penis-fencing". Two males hang face to face from a tree and rub their erect penises together. All members of the group have oral sex on occasion, massage each other's genitals, and kiss intensely. When adolescent females move over to another group for life the first thing they do is find an adult female and do some GG rubbing!

Even different groups will sometimes meet with each other and get it on. Why in the world would this be their way of life and survival? Well the explanation is that it reduces tension and conflict in the group. Even if a female hits a juvenile its mother may lunge at the aggressor but a minute later they will do some GG rubbing. Sex is also involved with obtaining food. When finding food they often first have a big orgy and then they settle down to eat. They certainly are an interesting bunch. The females rule and when they have boys the boys will stay with them all of their life for protection. Actually the most dominant males come from important mothers in the clan. What a life!

IF NOT FOR A LIGHTENING STRIKE WOULD AMERICA BE CHINESE

Of course the first people to discover the Americas were Asians crossing the Bering Strait over 13,000 years ago. They once again became the Indians of the Americas. In 986 C. E. the Viking Norwegian navigator Bjarni Herjolfsson tried to go to Greenland but wind and fog instead got him near the coast of North America. The winds then turned him back and he made it to Greenland. Around 1000 C. E. Leif Erikssin took Bjarni's boat and with 35 men headed westerly to North America. He probably knew that Bjarni had sighted an interesting forested area west of Greenland. They landed in today's Newfoundland. Due to the abundance there of the fox grape they named the area Vinlandia. They built houses and wintered in this area and then returned to Greenland. From the 1100s to the 1300s other journeys made it to this new land and they may at one time had 500 people living in this area. However, the native Indians were not real friendly and along with the potential of food problems and perhaps disease they were not able to permanently settle in this area. Then in the early 1400s the Northern Hemisphere experienced the "Little Ice Age" and no longer able to sustain themselves they even left Greenland for good. It is possible Christopher Columbus visited Iceland 15 years before his famous voyages and heard stories about this new land. Of course all American elementary kids know the story about Columbus discovering America. Too bad the story is all wet, but still it is nice to have a day off work for his holiday. He of course did take off on August 2, 1492 to find a short cut to China with his 3 ships. He landed in the Bahamas on October 12, 1492 and checked out the locals. Later during October he made it to Cuba and to Hispaniola (now Haiti). Again he was not real nice to the locals. He and his crews took off for Europe January 16, 1493 and they made it back on March 4, 1493. By the way he never made it to America on this or any other voyage. Figure that one out as far as Columbus Day is concerned. Now one may wonder if any other country made it to America in the 1400's? Could it have possibly have been the Chinese? Well, the Chinese for hundreds of previous years were culture wise way far ahead of Europe and any other area of the world. They were highly cultured, educated, and had huge armies. Of course they still had loads of peasants but they came in handy for all kinds of work. They also were masters of the sea with warships, freighters, and junks. They knew how to sail and understand longitudes and latitudes. They did have some previous problems. The Mongols had ruled most of China since 1279 by Kublai Khan, the grandson of Genghis Khan. But as so often is the case nature rules. A period of famines and floods caused havoc in China. Epidemics raged once again. The peasants finally revolted in 1352 and before long farmers and soldiers joined the good fight. Zhu Yuanzhang raised a big army and captured Nanjing. Before you knew it he took over the Mongol's capital Ta-tu that is now Beijing. This was the start of the 1st Ming Dynasty. He got kind of crazy right away as he had thousands of pre-puberty Mongol boys castrated to become Eunuchs. He did it up real good as he had both penises and testicles removed. This actually was a pretty common practice in many early societies. Anyway these eunuchs became servants, retainers, spies, harem-watchers, and even soldiers. 60,000 of them were retained in Beijing alone. A big-time job for some of them was to become harem-watchers since the Emperor had thousands of concubines partly to keep the dynasty in good shape. One eunuch Zheng He, was 6 foot 6 inches tall and weighed 220 pounds. He would soon become famous as a fighter and sailor. But before that happened Zhu Yuanzhang got old and died and one of his sons founded the 2nd Ming Dynasty. But before long turmoil in the family occurred and another son Zhu Di got an army of hundreds of thousands and soon took over the throne forming the 3rd Ming Dynasty. Zhu Di became the Son of Heaven and made Zheng He the Grand Eunuch. He soon named Zheng He commander-in-chief of a huge ocean fleet even though he had never sailed before. Before long a fleet of 3,000 - 4,000 vessels was formed. The fleet included large warships, treasure ships, junks, and freighters. They were soon to break up into groups and travel the world. All ships were highly advanced and the warships had gunpowder weapons, brass and iron cannon, mortars, flaming arrows, and exploding shells. They were to explore the oceans and both intimidate and impress other countries. On March 3, 1421 off they went and it appears they did indeed go all over the place. They went to India and both western and eastern Africa. They traveled over to South America and even took in Antarctica. They traveled to Australia in a number of different routes. They traveled up the western coast of South America and one fleet crossed the South Seas going to Australia and then up to the Philippines. Now what is interesting about this fleet is that the currents in June near the Philippines flow clockwise towards North America. Evidence suggests that they took these currents and landed on the Pacific coast of Canada. They then traveled down the California Current that took them down the California coast. Evidence suggests they landed in California and some of them may have stayed in this area for the rest of their lives. Of interest is that a wrecked Chinese junk dating to this era has been found off the coast of Oregon. Another medieval junk has been found inland buried in the Sacramento River. Carbon dating has affixed the date to the 1400's. It is possible that some Chinese sailors stayed and interbreed with the local native Indians. People later moving to these areas wrote of seeing pale Indians with the men having thick beards and the women having black hair. We have often found old pieces of pottery shaped in the Chinese style. So indeed it may have been possible that some sailors settled in this area in the 1400's. The rest of the fleet after going down the California coast then made it back to China in 1423. It is also possible that part of the Chinese fleet after being in the Caribbean traveled up to the coast of Florida and then up the eastern coast of America. The evidence for this is rather circumstantial but the 1st Europeans to go to New England encountered pale colored females who wore their hair in buns. What they also found growing was hops and rice which were not indigenous to this area. So once again perhaps they did make it to the Americas in the 1400's. What is kind of startling though is that it appears they did not land anywhere in Europe. Anyway what was left of the various fleets slowly made their way back to China in 1423. They had tons of interesting things to report about to the Emperor about their voyages and what the world was like. If things were well in China perhaps new and bigger voyages could be initiated and many of these new countries could be settled and dominated by the Chinese. Alas it was not to be. Two months after the fleets initially took sail in 1421 a horrendous violent storm hit Beijing. Lightening struck the Emperors palace, destroyed the concubine's center, and killed his favorite concubine through shock. Zhu Di lost it over the loss of his favorite squeeze. Zhu Di believed the gods had been mad at him and that they demanded a change in Emperor. Being a spiritual guy he temporarily handed it over to his son Zhu Gaozhi. He also wrote to his people that all things wrong in China were his fault and perhaps we can regain the favor of heaven. Well others in lower power blamed the fire and destruction of most of the palace on Zhu Di being too extravagant in his colossal building plans. Epidemics had also been raging in the south for 2 years killing more than 174,000 people. To keep things interesting Zhu Di had just had a number of strokes and was being treated with arsenic and mercury salts. To further compound his problems Vietnam was undergoing an uprising by Le L'oi. He would ultimately become the first ruler of a dynasty, which would last for 360 years. Even though China had a huge army Zhu Di was too ill and had lost much of his power to control the Vietnam situation. To add insult to injury the Mongols sensing that China was vulnerable refused to pay monetary tribute to China. Zhu Di established a force of almost 1 million men and tried to invade the Mongols but the expedition was a disaster. All in all China itself was now a disaster. This was the situation which the fleets encountered as they came back to China. It all started with that darn lightening strike on the palace. China slowly sunk back into smaller rural societies and the sailors never really got to exploit the fact that they could go back and take over many countries including America. America almost became Chinese! So it goes once again.

DO YOU HAVE THE RHYTHM

The ability to sing and or play musical instruments is a very complex brain activity, which is not receiving enough investigation. Currently we have not been able to find any definite genes which that wonderful singer or player possesses. However brain scan studies are attempting to at least quantify a little bit as to some of the brain areas involved with being a musician. It is highly probable that most humans inclined to become musicians have a genetic component directing brain neuron connections to areas involved with analytical processing of information. It is then up to their environmental upbringing as to how their growth proceeds in music. Investigations are coming into play where it is found that musicians tend to have left-sided brain dominance allowing them to relate music to an overall analytical process. They tend to interpret music more deeply than non-musicians. Non-musicians also tend to be more right-brain dominant. Musicians also tend to show increased blood flow velocity and volume in their left hemisphere. Of added interest is that musicians show a higher level of activation and size in an area of the brain called the left planum temporale. This area is well known to be involved with language and music. Of noted interest is that we can see the higher development of the left planum temporale even before a child is born who ultimately takes an interest in music. This helps show a genetic component is taking place. Now in regards to singing ability most likely genetic components exist mostly in regards to anatomical structure. One's vocal cords obtain a certain shape and size and even one's body shape may affect singing abilities. Our vocal cords consist of 2 skin-covered flaps of muscle that open and close across the passage to the lungs. They tend to oscillate with a wave motion as air rushes out during exhalation. Our larynx becomes the sound box sending the exhaled air into the singing sounds, which as we all know, can be pleasant or nasty. We are lucky in that we humans possess a larynx, which is low in our throat. This allows our tongue to have a greater freedom of movement giving us different sounds. As music teachers like to say we should sing with a relaxed larynx. With that to be said, lets take a look at an extremely gifted yet not so well known musician and singer who unfortunately left our world far too early. Gram Parsons was born in Winterhaven, Florida to wealthy parents in 1946. He had the proper anatomy and brain chemistry to become a gifted singer and guitar player starting his first band at the age of 12. In 1965 he attended Harvard University so he must have been pretty bright. But music was his thing and he joined the Byrds in 1968 but left them when they decided to tour in South Africa. He had other things in mine and formed the Flying Burrito Brothers in 1969. He was one of the first to develop what he called "Cosmic American Music". A great blend of country and rock his music needs to be listened to as many feel it is simply amazing. After the production of a number of albums he then teamed up with the unbelievable voice of Emmylou Harris forming The Fallen Angels. The harmonies of the 2 still bring shivers to those in the know! An album was made and off they went on The Fallen Angels tour in 1973. Emmylou Harris stated, "We set out to play country music and some rock & roll in the better hippie honky tonks of the nation". Unfortunately as is often the case with some musicians booze, drugs, and parties played a big part in his life. In 1968, a musical friend of his was killed by a drunk driver and after the funeral Gram stated this to a friend. "Phil, if this happens to me, I don't want them doing this to me. You can take me out to the desert and burn me. I want to go out in a cloud of smoke". Grams liked to go out to the Joshua Tree National Monument and hang out with nature. He would stay at the Joshua Tree Inn and there he was with 3 friends on September 17, 1973. Drinking Jack Daniels quite heavily he decided it was heroin time and before long it was in his system. He then topped that off with a bit of morphine. He overdosed but was revived with an ice cube suppository, an old street remedy. He recovered somehow and was soon walking around. However an hour or so later he passed out with labored breathing. He died. Traces of cocaine and barbiturates where found in his system. Soon to the rescue comes Phil Kaufman the road manager to such greats as the Rolling Stones, Frank Zappa, and Joe Cocker. Gram's body was to be flown from Los Angeles Airport to New Orleans and Phil had a mission to accomplish. He grabbed a hearse with no license plate and several broken windows and fueled with beer and Jack Daniels and a friend made it to the airport loading dock. Wearing cowboy boots, cowboy hats, and jackets with the legend "Sin City" on the back they actually told airport employees that family wanted them to ship the body back to New Orleans. Papers were signed and a police officer helped load the casket into the hearse. Strange days indeed! Off to the Joshua Tree Monument they went. They kept driving in the desert until they were too drunk to continue driving. They doused the body with gasoline and rapidly a fireball consumed the coffin. The semi-burned remains were soon found and shortly afterwards Phil and friend turned themselves into authorities. They were only charged with stealing a coffin and to pay off the fine he hosted a "Koffin Kaper Koncert". It turned out to be a memorable wake. Gram's remains are now buried in New Orleans in The Garden of Memories. His music survives and is one of the best of all on CDs.

A VERY COLD JANUARY

Without a doubt the most amazing event to occur during the history of humans was World War II. It was a time of impossibly to understand destruction and death. Nobody knows how many deaths occurred but it probably was over 60,000,000. Official Allied military deaths were estimated at 14,276,800 with

25,686,900 civilian deaths. The losing Axis powers had 6,582,000 military deaths and 1,686,000 civilians. Those figures would suggest that they Allies should have lost but it was just that the Germans and Japanese were tremendous killing machines in the early part of the war. Most humans do not know that there was 6 civilian deaths in the United States directly caused by the Japanese. The Japanese sent over to the United States and Canada over 9,000 large balloon bombs trying to intimidate and set fires to North America. Unfortunately on May 5, 1945 in Lakeview, Oregon a Mrs. Elsie Mitchell along with 5 neighborhood kids were killed as they dragged a bomb-loaded balloon not knowing it was dangerous. Of course a whole slew of books have been written about the worldwide conquests and campaigns. However one time period not well known to the casual reader was January of 1945 in Europe. Around Christmas of 1944 Hitler struck out at the thinly held Allied divisions in the famous Battle of the Bulge. My father was there and he has told me the story about it many a time. The Allied retreat was shocking to the world and it was not until late January when the Allies were able to retake the lost territory. Other than students of the war few know that the January of 1945 was the coldest in Europe in 40 years. Temperatures hovered between 0° - minus 10° or even colder. It snowed and the ground froze solid. Damp low clouds blew in from the North Sea where the Allies and Germans were fighting. Conditions were extremely windy and cold. In the case of the American soldiers a very serious problem existed. General Dwight D. Eisenhower and General Bradley had proceeded through Europe towards Germany at a very rapid pace after D-Day. It was possible the war might be over before Christmas. So his immense transport capabilities were invested in getting as much food, ammunition, gas, and other killing stuff to the front. What were not sent to a large degree were winter clothes and other wintertime type equipment. This created a tough situation for the soldier in the field. The soldiers just had leather boots, which easily became quite wet. Due to the extreme cold thousands of soldiers came down with trench foot. This is a rather generic term but the results can be devastating. Approximately 45,000 Allied solders had to be pulled out of the front line due to this malady. The real term for trench foot could be called "vasoneuropathy after prolonged chilling". In typical cases the soldiers first lost toenails and their feet turned white. Then the feet would turn purple and swollen and in severe cases necrosis (death) of tissue would happen. This would blacken the enlarged swollen feet. Of course intense pain would enter the equation. In the long run muscle and nerve damage may occur. The army in trying to lower incidences told the soldiers to constantly rub their feet and wear dry socks. The sock thing was difficult since they usually only had a couple of pairs and the foxholes etc were wet. So they would take off the wet socks and wrap them around their neck and take the somewhat dry ones from their neck and put them on. It was a constant cycle of sorts. It's too bad the soldiers did not have antiperspirants handy as studies show they reduce foot sweating and thereby reduce trench foot incidents. Now trench foot certainly was bad but when the freezing conditions came about in Germany many soldiers developed actual frostbite. In this condition the skin tissue actually freezes. If one could not leave his position then the cold goes deeper into the body damaging the muscles, tendons, joints, and even the bones. Hemorrhagic bleeding, ulceration, and gangrene often occurred. In countless cases amputation was needed. At least this got many soldiers out of the European field of operation, which got really nasty in January. Things were far from being over as far as the war was concerned. General Eisenhower had 73 divisions at his disposal but the Germans had 76 divisions. Yes it is true that some of the German soldiers were very young or older men. But some of them were crack divisions who were very battle hardy. Unfortunately the Allied divisions had many new raw recruits. It was the American policy to not relieve entire divisions weary from battle. Instead as soldiers were killed or wounded in a division new recruits just arriving from the United States would be just thrown into the division to keep adequate numbers of soldiers. Many of these young soldiers only made it a few days before their number was up. Even though the conditions were extreme Eisenhower launched mighty attacks north and south of what was once the bulge. The Germans still occupied much of the territory they seized in their December attacks. His rationales were rather complex but he was worried that V-1 and V-2 rocket attacks were hitting London and the port city of Antwerp. He also knew German fighter planes were coming on line and they of course were much faster than any Allied plane. During the main attacks 300,000 Allied soldiers were involved and they seldom had help from the Air Force since conditions were seldom conducive for flying in January. The men were tired, cold, and thousands were sick from the conditions. In many areas there was over a foot of snow and the roads were frozen and slick. The German 88's continually pounded the roads limiting travel. As the soldiers slowly made their way through the woods and fields they would remove their heavy overcoats and blankets hoping that trucks would pick them up later to be delivered back before night fall. Sometimes the soldiers were fortunate and spent the night in the basement of destroyed houses. Quite often it was a long night in a foxhole. During the daytime the movement was slow and moving a few hundred yards a day was the rule. In some sectors of the battles each side on a daily basis put off over 10,000 artillery rounds. To compound the issue Hitler wanted to hold the gains of the Bulge and he also wanted an offensive move towards Alcase to keep new Allied troops from coming into the battles. Fortunately he was unsuccessful in this endeavor and by January 21, 1945 he stopped his divisions short of Alcase. By the end of January the Allies had pushed the Germans back to where the Allies were before the Bulge. The casualties show the degree of warfare during the month of January. The United States had 6,138 killed with 27,262 wounded in battle. The Germans suffered 80,000 – 104,000 killed and wounded. February did come about and although it was not as cold, constant rain and mud became the new issue.

IT IS GOOD TO HAVE A LIVER

In order to stay healthy humans need a properly functioning liver. It is our largest gland weighing about 3 pounds in the average adult. It has lots of jobs to perform on a daily basis. It produces bile and lecithin which aides in digestion. It not only stores glucose sugar but also converts dietary fructose to glucose that is our main sugar to be made into energy. The liver carries on most of the fat synthesis going on in the body and also makes cholesterol. Our liver breaks down amino acids from proteins and removes ammonia-like poisons for elimination by the kidneys. It also synthesizes most of the proteins of the blood plasma. It helps to convert provitamin D to real vitamin D. It stores the fat-soluble vitamins and especially vitamin B_{12} that is needed to make red blood cells. It stores and regulates iron usage in the blood, which is big for energy production. Our liver is also involved in the production of at least 5 hormones and various clotting factors. Of extreme importance is that it is the major filter of the constant amounts of poisons (xenobiotics), which we take into us on a daily basis. These once again are the nasty free radicals already discussed somewhat in previous thoughts. The livers job is to neutralize the poisons so that the kidneys can then eliminate them out in the urine. So to say the least if the liver fails that's it for that individual human. Our liver may become damaged by a host of different mechanisms. These include both hepatitis B and C infections. Excessive alcohol intake, iron overload, and even an accumulation of toxic chemicals may insult the liver over time. Various pharmaceutical medicines may further damage the liver. The potential damage to the liver from these sources may lead to cirrhosis or cancer. Cirrhosis of the liver is rather easy to explain. The good liver hepatic cells die and are replaced with scar tissue. Scar tissue does not function well and the liver fails to perform its duties. Primary liver cancer affects more males than females and may also be caused by the above mechanisms. Even people with cirrhosis often develop primary liver cancer. It is actually the 5th most common cancer in the world. Primary liver cancer typically starts as a tumor but since it is usually not painful the patient does not know they have it until it has advanced to other areas of the liver. That is certainly too bad because in the early stage surgery can remove the tumor and the patient often is cured. Unfortunately most people are diagnosed in a more advanced stage and then the outlook is not so good. Survival rates are then very low and not many survive more than a year or 2 depending on individual circumstances. So it should be obvious that one should avoid both cirrhosis and liver cancer. Do not get hepatitis and avoid as many free radical poisons as possible. Keep up with the antioxidant intake. Make sure about the medicines one takes as they may cause liver damage. Alcohol intake is actually kind of an interesting association. Most individuals that consume moderate levels of alcohol never get cirrhosis and some who never drink do get it. Actually we now are aware that having a fatty liver may lead to cirrhosis. Actually consuming small amounts of alcohol may be healthful for many individuals. It raises the good HDL cholesterol levels and lowers blood pressure somewhat. It also thins the blood. Excessive consumption most certainly harms many and this is especially true if they have a bad diet. Studies show that drinkers who consume many vitamins and minerals often suffer little liver damage. But by far the best thing one can do to preserve liver function is to consume on a daily basis the herb milk thistle. Milk thistle (*Siylbum marianus*) is a fairly large invasive plant found in the daisy family and it has a long medical history. It has been used for many years in the European community where herbs are often prescribed before modern medicines. From the seeds we extract a number of flavonoids known as silymarin. When one takes the herbal capsules the ingredients soon make it to the liver. It is extremely nontoxic and is wonderful for the liver cells. In the liver it acts as an antioxidant neutralizing many poisons including the poisonous acetaldehyde generated from alcohol breakdown. It protects the liver cells by keeping free radical reactions from damaging the cell membrane of these cells. It keeps poisons from entering the cells and helps to remove them from the liver for elimination. Silymarin also boosts liver protein synthesis so that liver cells can better repair themselves. It is the liver's "best friend". To show its potential just look at the individuals who have encountered extreme liver damage from drinking alcohol and taking to much acetaminophen. What can happen in this scenario is that too many free radicals are produced and the liver becomes damaged. Companies like Tylenol even list this as a potential possibility on their label. Well we now know that consuming milk thistle will neutralize the effects of these 2 chemicals and the liver will not be damaged. To take this somewhat to the extreme try to recall how the death cap mushroom (*Amanita phalloides*) can kill you just by eating a nice juicy one. Well in Germany if you eat that mushroom and just start to get sick you can go to a hospital. There they will infuse you with liquid silymarin and the liver will receive little damage. Once again silymarin is the liver's "best friend"! Too bad for you if you live in the U.S. since the FDA has not approved its use. You just die a painful death unless you fly real fast to Germany. So on a daily basis it is wise to take 1,000 mg or so of this useful herb. It actually is best absorbed into the body in an alcohol base so feel free to have a beer with it.

OVER 2 MILLION DEATHS

It is pretty weird that the lack of an electron can cause over 2 million deaths during the "age of sail". This was the time period when European countries sent sailors throughout the world for exploration, colonization, exploitation, and to generally terrify people. For the captains and the bigwigs on board conditions on many of the ships was tolerable. However for the general sailor conditions were typically pretty darn ruff. For example the largest battleships in the 1600's weighed 2,500 tons and were about 300 feet long. It may have carried 120 big guns and the ship held over 1,000 men. In fact up to 500 men would sleep in hammocks in compartments 50 feet wide and 150 feet long. Being out in the oceans for months at a time was tough work and the food was far from good. Typically the food often consisted of salt beef, salt pork, and salted fish, which had been in storage for some time. Sailors also ate lots of butter, cheese, dried peas, dried apples, and pears. Of course sugar was around and sometimes raisins, and barley meal. The highlight of the day was the beer that sometimes was up to a gallon a day. The grog was better than the stored water that was around which soon got putrid. They did not know about bleach in those days. All in all conditions typically were damp and much of the food would go bad yet was still needed to be consumed. It is easy to understand that sailors were afflicted with all kinds of illnesses during their journeys. There existed little in the way of sound medical help during the voyages and many sailors were buried at sea. Due to the various illnesses and nasty conditions it is easy to appreciate that the worst illness of all during the voyages was totally misunderstood. It has been estimated once again that over 2 million sailors died from the dreaded scurvy. In fact for many years approximately 50% of some crews died slowly from this deficiency disease. That is one of the reasons many ships were overloaded with sailors at the beginning of the voyage. After a couple months at sea some of the sailors would get extremely tired and their teeth would get very loose and their gums would start to bleed. Bruising would soon occur all over the body, as the internal blood vessels would break down. As the days went on the color of the skin would look terrible and within time it became impossible to eat and to even sit up. Death from organ failure would occur and if the body was autopsied the inner organs looked like a bunch of mush. Scurvy had caused all of the connective tissue in the body to literally break apart. Since connective tissue is the glue that holds our organs, blood vessels, and tissues together the human just sort of suffered a total "meltdown". Of course today we know all about the problem and how to remedy the situation but in the old days they had no clue. As already noted we need a small amount of vitamin C in order to prevent scurvy. Vitamin C once again donates an electron to iron atoms, which activates the enzyme that keeps our connective tissue healthy. Once our vitamin C reserves run out then no more electron donation and the body falls apart. Of course this seldom happens on land since we tend to consume fruits and veggies supplying us with some vitamin C. But those poor souls on board ships for months received hardly any vitamin

C from the types of foods, which could be stored at sea for long periods of times. There was no way anyone during that time period had a clue about either connective tissue or vitamin C. So for hundreds of years the deaths kept occurring even when unproven methods were used to contain the disaster. They tried good old bloodletting that was an obvious failure. Adding hydrochloric acid to their drinking water did not cut it nor did putting mercury on their wounds. They tried vinegar and oil of vitriol. Oil of vitriol is actually sulfuric acid and how that would help is beyond this chemist. Actually they used the stuff for all kinds of silly reasons since it was available. They would just take sulfur and potassium nitrate and in the presence of steam one makes sulfuric acid. It is unfortunate but medicine in Europe was pretty much a bunch of quackery due to a lack of scientific principles. Too bad the Internet wasn't around in 1535 because North American Indians already knew the cure for scurvy. Under the command of Jacques Cartier about 100 Frenchmen found themselves having to spend the winter near what is now Quebec City in a primitive fort. They did not quite make it to the Spice Islands by this northern route. They only had old rations from their 3 ships, which were devoid of vitamin C. Scurvy soon took hold with many too sick to walk. However one group was able to leave and visit a nearby Iroquois settlement where everyone was quite healthy. When these sailors came back a week or so later Cartier noticed that one guy named Dom Agaya was well and all healed from the scurvy he had before the Indian visit. Of course Cartier wanted to know the cure and so Agaya with 2 female Iroquois went to the woods and brought back 10 – 12 branches of the white cedar tree. They boiled the leaves into a drink and the rest of Cartier's sick sailors drank the concoction for 6 days. Low and behold they got better and the rest of the winter it was white cedar tea as often as possible. They sailed home in the summer but the word really never got out to the European sailing communities. It would take a couple hundred more years to figure out the solution. In 1739 at the age of 23 James Lind entered the Royal Navy as a young doctor. He soon saw the affects of the dreaded scurvy and actually tried a controlled experiment on some shipmates. He wondered if it could be cured using various substances. He divided the group into 7 pairs. One pair already had advanced scurvy and they just got their regular food and grog. All of the other groups also got their normal rations. However group 1 was given cider (with a little alcohol) and group 2 was given 25 drops of oil of vitriol (sulfuric acid) daily on an empty stomach. I am sure the sulfuric acid was not 18 molar, which is a chemist's joke! Anyway group 3 was given 2 spoonfuls of vinegar 3 times a day and group 4 got a half-pint of sea water per day. Lind wanted to try seawater since if it worked there was a lot available for the crew. The 5th group received 2 oranges plus 1 lemon during the experiment. The 6th group got all kinds of interesting tidbits. On a daily basis they got paste of nutmeg, garlic, mustard seed, dried radish root, balsam of peru (resin from the balsam tree), and gum myrrh. All groups were purged daily with cream of tartar. Well to keep it short only those receiving the oranges and lemons avoided the scurvy. Actually the group with the advanced scurvy soon died. The 6th group got all kinds of stuff but none of it contained vitamin C. Lind finally published his data 6 years later and he then wrote in 1753 a book titled "Treatise on the Scurvy, containing an inquiry into the nature, causes, and cure, of that disease together with a critical and chronological view of what has been published on the subject". That sure sounds good but he blew it big time because in this 400-page book he generally said that scurvy is due to a blockage by the body's natural perspiration that leads to an imbalance in the body's alkalinity. He thought scurvy was made worse by the damp conditions at sea. He did state that oranges and lemons would work but he thought acids such as oil of vitriol would be just as good. Its too bad he really did not just say oranges and lemons would do the trick. His work was soon forgotten as other weird cures were being investigated on board other ships. Then in 1768 the famous captain James Cook led an English voyage to the South Pacific. He made sure his ships stayed clean and tried to stop as often as possible to gather fresh fruits and veggies. He even kept on board sauerkraut, wild onions, wild celery, and scurvy grass. All of these contain small amounts of vitamin C. Scurvy grass is in the cabbage family and grows in salty marshes. In 1775 he made it back to England reporting no cases of scurvy. But still nobody really associated fresh fruits and veggies directly with scurvy. Of a side note Cook made it to Hawaii and overstayed his welcome in 1779. He got into a fight with the natives and they stabbed and drowned him and then cut him up. Fortunately I guess the natives gave his crew back some of his body parts and he was later buried at sea. Well life progresses on and by 1783 England had 430 warships and 107,446 men on board them. But England by now was due for an attack from the combined French – Spanish fleet. The English crews were suffering from scurvy since they kept out to sea defending the English coast. Along came the French – Spanish fleet but the Spanish fleet was 7 weeks late due to weather and scurvy abounded on their ships. Even two-thirds of the Frenchies had the scurvy and the whole fleet had to retreat without battle. Perhaps history was changed by scurvy once again. Soon however things were going to start to get better as far as the scurvy. In 1781 Gilbert Blane became the personal physician to Admiral Sir George Rodney. He ultimately became the physician for the entire fleet. He read about Linn's book and also about the voyages of James Cook. A light must have lit up in his head as he believed that oranges, lemons, and limes would stop the scurvy. He ultimately had his Admirals give two-thirds of an ounce of lemon juice with 2 ounces of sugar to the sailors on a daily basis. By the early 1800's the Royal Navy was consuming 50,000 gallons of lemon juice annually. From 1795 – 1814 more than 1.6 million gallons of the stuff went on the Royal Navy ships. It took hundreds of years and untold lives but scurvy rates all but disappeared. Too bad the Chinese back in 1421 had that violent lightening strike on Zhu Di's palace leading to the decline of China. When the Chinese fleet came back in 1423 they could have told the world they already had a cure for scurvy. As those fleets went around the world they carried limes, lemons, pomelos (like a grapefruit), and coconuts. They also buried bamboo shoots and grapes in sand to keep them fresh. They sprouted soya beans during their journeys, which were high in vitamin C. Scurvy was not a problem for their crews but the word never got out. Did 2 million sailors die due to a lightening strike in 1421? Of a final note how in the world do Eskimos up north not get scurvy since in the past few fruits and veggies were available? The answer lies in liver and raw meat. A liver is able to store some vitamin C and for thousands of year's seals, fish, and other ocean animals were the major food staple. They always ate the liver and their meat raw just as they liked eyeballs so they avoided scurvy by eating tasty livers and almost raw meat. Raw meat also contains small amounts of vitamin C.

SMOKUM IF YOU GOTUM

It is somewhat amusing that governments take one of the world's most dangerous substances and make it legal to purchase. We are talking of course about the cigarette, which is the number one cause of unnecessary deaths worldwide. The rationale involves history but of course it is a big money maker. It is a huge commodity and so of course is good for economies. It is often heavily taxed providing governmental money. It also helps keep doctors and hospitals in business. Too bad it is more addictive in nature than heroin. *Nicotiana tabacum* is the most common species of tobacco used by the cigarette industry. It is in the potato family, *(Solanaceae)* which includes many poisonous species. Native to the Western Hemisphere it was smoked by Pre-Columbians for its hallucinogenic effects as early as 1 B.C.E. When Columbus arrived he was given it as a gift and was smoked in an instrument made of stone called a tabaca. Here is where the Europeans picked up the word tobacco. The complex genetics of this plant causes it to synthesize in its cells a wide assortment of complicated hydrocarbons that we call tars. It also synthesizes nicotine ($C_{10}H_{14}N_2$), which of course is the addicting substance. Actually over 4,000 chemicals have been isolated from tobacco including over 40 cancer causing substances. To make matters worse the tobacco roots readily absorb arsenic, cadmium, lead, chromium, and nickel. Radioactive particles are also taken into the plant from the soils in which the plants are grown. These include radium, thorium, and especially polonium[210]. With every cig you smoke you inhale radiation, which hardly anyone is aware of and of course is not listed by the companies. You even inhale formaldehyde with which we preserve dead humans. Of interest is that the plant produces nicotine in order to kill insects that might feed on the plant. It is a strong poison in which 2 or 3 drops of it would kill you if you select this method of your demise. So what's up with smoking the stuff? Curiously enough the nicotine molecule closely resembles a major brain chemical known as acetylcholine. This is the primary neurotransmitter molecule that goes across the synapse space between brain neurons stimulating millions of brain activities. Nicotine easily fits into what are called nicotinic-acetylcholine receptors that normally respond to acetylcholine. That's a weird biochemical similarity to have but that is just the way it goes. When the nicotine from smoking goes into the receptors it stimulates certain brain electrical pathways causing changes in the brain. Reaction time and attention span are increased and anxiety, appetite, and even pain are somewhat decreased. Our brain metabolizes glucose as an energy source faster after a smoke. The reward pathway is also stimulated and small amounts of dopamine are produced which is our pleasure molecule. Unfortunately the effects are short-lived so the brain starts making more nicotinic-acetylcholine receptors and the smoker tends to need more nicotine in order to continue the all around reward seeking pathways. Depending upon a number of factors including cigarette consumption the vast majority of smokers ultimately become hooked as they say. In fact new and interesting research is showing that addiction levels may be somewhat controlled by our genetics. We now are aware that a gene named CHRNA4 exists that regulates the development of the nicotinic-acetylcholine receptors in the brain. One gene variant of CHRNA4, which we may inherit, causes the nicotine to become highly active when locked into the receptor. This means those with that gene get a stronger overall stimulus from the nicotine such as more dopamine production and more overall awareness. They tend to become addicted to a higher level making it much harder to want to or be able to stop smoking. Of added interest we are now aware that an unknown chemical in cigarette smoke actually keeps dopamine levels relatively high for extended periods. This substance keeps an enzyme known as monoamine oxidase B from destroying dopamine in the brain so the pleasure experience lasts longer. Withdrawal symptoms of course vary by the individual but are highly biological in nature. Not receiving the dopamine pleasing effects in fact are pretty much psychological. However nicotine affects many brain pathways and a sudden lack of it can cause serious disturbances. For example nicotine stimulates a pathway that slows down the production of serotonin in the hippocampus area of the brain. This area is involved with anxiety and stress in humans and by slowing serotonin production one feels less stress and anxiety. However the brain reacts to the lower serotonin levels by producing more serotonin receptors in the hippocampus. When one stops smoking soon the hippocampus area produces large amounts of serotonin. Since this area now contains more receptors, higher than normal amounts of serotonin induces stress and anxiety in the person trying to quit. Nicotine also activates areas in the brain to stimulate the adrenal glands to produce adrenalin. Adrenalin as is well known makes our body more aware and alert. When one quits smoking the adrenals are not activated due to the nicotine and this leads to lethargy. One has to remember that every time you smoke adrenalin is produced and the body gets used to this slight rush. Finally we are aware that an area in the brain known as the insula processes emotional experiences such as cravings that have developed over time. Nicotine is involved in this area and a lack of it elicits the cigarette cravings. This has been shown to be true by studying humans who have suffered a brain injury to this area. Doctors have found that those who suffer injury to the insula, and those who smoke, immediately lose the urge and desire to smoke. They quit right away and do not take up the habit again. So indeed with the psychological problems of quitting there exists a real big physiological problem with quitting. It is however of obvious importance that one should certainly kick this habit. It is the number 1 cause of avoidable deaths in the modern world. Heart disease, cancer, and strokes are the major causes of death in modern societies. This certainly occurs in non-smokers but smoking incredibly increases their overall risk to those humans. Smoking also increases the risk of emphysema, obstructive pulmonary disease, and a whole slew of lesser-known problems. The problem lies in the gases and the tars that are released with each inhalation. Combusting (smoking) the cigarette sends into the lungs and bloodstream incredibly horrible substances. It is sort of like taking the liquid tar found on our roads on a hot day and putting it in a pipe to smoke. Of course that's taking it a little too far but when the tars are ignited in cigarettes they rapidly turn into free radicals that go far throughout the body. It is the job of our liver to neutralize them and have them excreted out in our wastes. It is simply amazing that our liver has enzymes that can somewhat keep up with the neutralization process. But the enzymes in the liver of smokers are constantly in overdrive and slowly but assuredly all are not neutralized and the free radical damage begins affecting our circulatory system and organs. Unfortunately we have all inherited differing enzymatic neutralizing systems in our liver and cells. Some work better than others. To further complicate the issue humans possess a gene whose function is to monitor whether a cell in our body is working properly or becoming pre-cancerous. This gene is well known and called the p53 tumor suppressor gene and we all have inherited a variation of it. If one has inherited an abnormal p53 gene it is readily damaged by cigarette smoke making this person at high risk for lung cancer. Approximately 95% of people who get lung cancer are smokers. Currently a simple test as to which variant one has inherited is not available. So once again it is simply silly to smoke cigarettes but it is also hard as shown to stop. One may ask if there is anything out there on the horizon making it easy to stop. Well with all of the millions of dollars invested in finding an easy way to stop from a molecular level the answer is no. However, here might be a method, which might work and is currently being investigated. Most cigarettes deliver 1 – 2 mgs of nicotine and light cigarettes are no better than the stronger varieties. Humans just tend to inhale deeper with the light varieties, which just gives them lung cancer deeper down in the lungs. That by the way is a fact! However if you want to quit you might want to try the low – nicotine cigs that only deliver 0.02 mgs of nicotine. When you get those cigs go to your local doctor and ask for a prescription for mecamylamine (Inversine) at a 2.5 – 5 mg dosage. Mecamylamine was one of the first medicines available to treat blood pressure. It had some problems at the dosage given to reduce blood pressure and is seldom used. Studies are being conducted to see if this lower dosage may really help you quit smoking. This medicine readily goes through our blood-brain barrier and sticks into our acetylcholine-nicotinic receptors. This keeps most but not all of the nicotine from the low – nicotine cigarettes from stimulating its normal pathways. Ultimately the desire and need to smoke goes away. Give it a try because you only have your health to worry about!

STEPHEN HAWKING AND BLACK HOLES

Some humans are just way too smart. Such was the case for Sir Isaac Newton (1643 – 1726). He was a mathematician, physicist, astronomer, philosopher, and a theologian. He actually wrote more on religion than anything else. But he did write in 1687 the *Philosophioe Naturalis Principia Mathematica,* that may be one of the earth's greatest works in science. He generally invented the calculus, which is the mathematics of the universe. In this text he described gravitation and the 3 laws of motion. He invented the reflecting telescope and showed that the prism decomposes white light into visible colors. He showed how gravity affected the orbits of our planets. At Cambridge he was elected Lucasian Professor of Mathematics and became the President of the Royal Society in 1703. He is buried in Westminster Abbey, which is something in itself. Then in the 20th century along comes Stephen Hawking. He is another real smart guy. Born in 1942 in Oxford, England he attended University College, Oxford to study physics. He actually wanted to study mathematics but it was not available at this part of Oxford. Upon graduating with honors he went to Cambridge to study cosmology and received his Ph.D. At the age of 32, he was named a fellow of the Royal society. He received the Albert Einstein Award, the most prestigious in theoretical physics. In 1979 he was appointed Lucasian Professor of Mathematics and Cambridge which chair he still holds. I told you he is one smart guy! He is still working on the basic laws that govern the universe. He has shown that Einstein's General Theory of Relativity shows that space and time started in the Big Bang. He is really into the concept of black holes. His accomplishments are amazing for a man who came down with amylotrophic lateral sclerosis (ALS) when in his 20's. This is one of the most horrible disorders that exist and most people only live a couple of years after it is diagnosed. In ALS the motor neurons, which allow movement of our muscles die. During the early stages only the neurons going to the voluntary muscles die. The patient progressively becomes paralyzed. Then in most cases but not all the neurons going to the involuntary muscles die. These muscles are the ones, which causes for example our lungs to expand and contract. Death soon follows. Science is getting a grip on what the cause of this disorder is all about but no cure is in sight. ALS is all about those nasty free radicals and in this disorder the radicals are made in our body. We all know we need oxygen to survive. What is not so well known is that nature has made a big goof up in every plant and animal cell. The mitochondria is the area in cells where sugars are burned into energy with the use of oxygen. For an unknown reason in the complicated pathway of making energy 2 out of every 100 oxygen molecules picks up an extra electron. It becomes a reactive superoxide free radical. This radical will then seek another electron so that it can become stable. So it rips electrons from the proteins, sugars, and fats in our cells. Even our DNA may slowly be damaged in time. Superoxide free radicals are actually one of the major causes of the aging process since slow damage to our mitochondria slows down the activities of our cells. It is one of the main reasons why people in their 70's and 80's can not do the things they did at an earlier age. Fortunately antioxidants can neutralize free radicals and we even have enzymes that can neutralize them. A major enzyme is superoxide dimutase and it is made by all of our cells and it functions to make superoxide free radicals into harmless water. It needs both zinc and copper attached to it for it to be activated. Here is the problem with ALS. For some reason an altered gene causes the superoxide dimutase enzymatic protein to take on a new structural look and zinc atoms cannot attach to the enzyme. The enzyme does not become activated and superoxide free radicals are then not destroyed. In the case of ALS the superoxide free radicals accumulate and they destroy the neurons allowing muscle movement. These radicals damage certain proteins in the neurons causing them to die. Fortunately for the world Stephen Hawking's ALS stopped at the stage where only his voluntary muscles neurons were destroyed. His involuntary muscles have continued to function and although paralyzed he has been able to continue his quests in cosmology. When dealing with black holes he is the master. The concept of the existence of black holes actually was theorized in Cambridge way back in 1783. Black holes are really about escape velocity. Escape velocity is sort of like thinking about the space shuttle. In order to make it out of our atmosphere it must go 25,054 mph. The escape velocity from our sun is 1,382,464 mph, which seems a lot but since light travels at 670,000,000 mph it easily escapes and we see things. But what if the escape velocity from a massive star is greater than the speed of light? Well of course Hawking says that light would be dragged back by the gravity of the star. So it goes something like this. When this massive star burns up its hydrogen fuel it explodes into a supernova. The stuff that is left over collapses down to an extremely dense object called a neutron star. Soon the gravitational forces overwhelm the pressure gradients and the collapse cannot be halted. The neutron star continues to shrink until it becomes a black hole. As all of this is happening any light being given off will not be able to have enough escape velocity to leave. The light will be bent back inward by the curvature of spacetime. Most people believe that nothing can escape being sucked into a black hole but if that were true the black holes of the universe would have pretty much sucked in a lot of galaxies. Fortunately there exists what is known as the "event horizon". This is the area where the black hole starts to exert its sucking in ability. Outside of the "event horizon" things are status quo and any forms of mass or light will not be drawn into the black hole. In theory if our sun became a black hole (which it cannot) the "event horizon" would not even cause our planets to leave their orbits. So how do we know black holes exist since we cannot see them? According to Hawking all we have to do is look out into space. He has shown that a black hole still exerts a gravitational pull on its neighboring objects as it did when it was a sun. So all scientists have to do is look through our new telescopes and find objects that are orbiting around some not to be seen object. Indeed, scientists have already found many black holes. For example in 2006 one was found 10 times as massive as our sun in the elliptical galaxy NGC 4472, located 50 million light-years away. We have also found 3 supermassive black holes in 2006 using the new European Space Observatory's Very Large Telescope. They are located 10.5 billion light-years away in the Virgo constellation. What is really neat is that these black holes have monstrous quasars by them. So what in the world is a quasar? We should know about them as we have spotted over 100,000 of them in the universe and they are incredibly bright. Actually some of them are 1 trillion times as bright as our sun. They are even larger than our solar system. Astronomers believe that quasars are far distant galaxies that are powered by supermassive rotating black holes that suck in gaseous matter from the galaxy. So it is amazing the knowledge being gained about our universe and Stephen Hawking has been a major theorist in our understanding of the universe. We can only hope that he has many more years on earth.

THE ISLAMIC RELIGION

Currently there are around 1.2 billion Muslims and the faith is growing at a rate of 2.9% a year. From a personal standpoint I tutored the son of a Muslim family for 10 years. His mother was one of the kindest women I ever met and she was very religious in her faith. The father was a secular type guy. Currently as is well known the Islamic religion is receiving all kinds of publicity and a worldwide stage. So what is this religion all about? It is all about Muhammad who was an Arab living in the Middle East in the 7th century C.E. For Muslims, Muhammad is indeed the final prophet of Allah (God) and it was he that delivered the final and perfect word of God. He was born about 570 C.E. with the name Muhammad Ibne Abdullah in Mecca. During this time period Mecca and the surrounding region was full of semi-warring tribes with differing polytheistic religions. Allah was considered to be the supreme deity but not the only one. At the age of 6 his mother died and so his grandfather then raised him. But then he died and his uncle Abu Talib then took over the responsibility. He was a businessman and Mohammad went with him on many trips. On these journeys he encountered many Jews and Christians. Around the age of 35 he liked to head out to nearby Mount Hira to relax and contemplate life. He liked to meditate in a cave and one day an angel appeared to him. Soon thereafter he said the angel Gabriel appeared to him and told him to start reciting stuff. So he did for many years and this became the Qur'an (Koran). He kept seeing the angel and other times he heard bells and intense lights. It is note worthy to suggest that perhaps he was another one of those suffering from Temporal Lobe Epilepsy. He was said to have had fits as a child and may have been born with excess brain fluid. Anyway he kept reciting verse for 23 years until he died in 632 C.E. Since he could not read nor write he had others jot down what he had to say. He believed he was the messenger of God, sent forth to confirm previous scriptures. He believed in a monotheistic faith and said that God did reveal his will to the Jews and the Christians through chosen apostles. But he felt both religions disobeyed God's commandments. The Jews he believed

corrupted the scriptures. The Christians believed of course that
Jesus was the son of God. To Muhammad God commanded that
nobody worship anybody other than him. Muhammad stressed
that both groups must be brought back to the true religion
preached by Abraham. This became Islam, which is the absolute
submission or resignation to the will of God. Muhammad's God
is compassionate and forgiving but also stern in retribution. He
seeks justice, fair dealing, kindness to orphans and widows, and
charity to the poor. One may be saved and enter Paradise which is
full of sensual pleasures. The day of Judgement will come and
men will be weighed on that day. Those that have done good
deeds will be fine but the unsaved will go to Hell. Muslims
believe in the literal word of the Quar'an, which unbelievers may
find to be an interesting text. It is full of all kinds of quotes and
words from Moses, Abraham, and Joseph. This is kind of
interesting since they had been dead a long time ago. The
Quar'an does contain many positive notes. For example;
"Believers Jews, Christians, and Sabaeans – whoever believes in
God and the last day and does what is right, - shall be rewarded by
their lord; they have nothing to fear or regret". "Whatever you
bestow in charity must go to the parents and to kinsfolk, to the
orphans and to the helpless and to the traveler in need. God is
aware of whatever good you do". On the other hand some phrases
highlight a different note. For example: "Men have authority over
women because God has made the one superior to the other, and
because they spend their wealth to maintain them. Good women
are obedient. As for those from whom you fear disobedience,
admonish them and send them to beds apart and beat them".
"You will find that the most implacable of men in their enmity to
the faithful are the Jews and the pagans, and that in the nearest in
affection to them are those who say: we are the Christians".
Believers, take neither Jews nor Christians for your friends. God
does not guide the wrongdoers". It is no wonder the world still
harbors many religious problems. But for now lets get back to
Muhammad. When he died he had 12 wives, which is interesting
in itself. But who was to replace him and keep Islam functioning?

Well at the beginning he was replaced by caliphs (leader of the Muslims) to whom he was not related. When the 3rd one, Uthman, was murdered while at prayer he was replaced by Ali. He was a cousin of Muhammad and was married to his daughter Fatima. Soon things did not go well as various fractions did not want Ali as caliph. A battle ultimately ensued and Ali was killed by one of his own men. A guy named Mu'awiya became caliph but a young son of Ali named Ali survived and tried to continue the Ali line. A schism sort of happened with two sides of Muslims dividing away from each other. One group is the Sunnis, which makes up about 85% of current Muslims. The other group is the Shi'a (Shites), which makes up the other 15%. Their differences go way back to the death of Muhammad. The Sunnis believe that the first 4 caliphs rightfully took the place of Muhammad as their leader. The Shi'a on the other hand believe that only the heirs of the 4th caliph, Ali, are the true successors of Muhammad. They both essentially believe the same Islamic fundamentals. They do have some differences such as believing in different interpretations of the Hadith. This is a collection of works written about the life of Muhammad. The Sunnis feel the Shi'a dwell too much on the martyrdom of Ali. The Shi'a feel they are the true successors to the "house of Mohammad. Throughout the years both groups have fought and at other times got along rather well. One must remember that the Arab population in general has been organized into many loose groups of tribal people. As a result there have been constant quarrels among rival factions. This of course has been shown in the horrible situation in Iraq in which the minority Sunnis had power over the Shi'a majority. This happened due to the power of the Saddam Hussein dynasty. Currently as we speak the country is now occupied by a number of Islamic fractions fighting for control. The Shi'a dominated Iran is hard at play making things more unsettling in this area of the world. Lebanon is currently being divided by the Shi'a political party, known as the Hezbollah. This group is backed by Syria and is against the Sunni led government. Only time will tell when matters will settle in the entire Middle East. Oh yes do not forget

that the Muslims still do not like the Jews! Perhaps the Muslims
should just settle back and enjoy a glass of wine with each other.
Their major vices today are cigarettes, tea, and strong coffee.
Actually Muhammad enjoyed his wine and the Qur'an does not
explicably say no to alcohol. The ban is actually attributed to a
collection of hadiths of Al-Bukari (810-870). In one hadith a
story goes that the 2nd caliph Umar al-Khattab (634 – 644 C.E.)
was given a bottle of wine but did not know what to do with it?
So the Prophet said, "Go outside and smash the bottles on a
stone". So in general the consumption of alcohol is a big no!
Kids are taught this early in life along with the other no's such as
gambling. Unfortunately many are being taught that America is
the big Satan and we are infidels. Extremism, although not the
norm, is rapidly gaining momentum. Literally thousands of young
are being hard-wired at early ages to mount a crusade against the
west. If this is all that you are taught then your brain chemistry
will develop a brain that most humans cannot understand. It is
sort of like the American child who is constantly told early in life
that whites are the superior race. To them this becomes the norm
but hopefully as they become educated in society they will gain a
better understanding of all humans. Unfortunately for many poor
Muslims receiving only a narrow-minded education it will be very
difficult for most to change.

BLACKS ARE USUALLY BROWNS

Recently a student of mine got a pass from the office and I
asked her what she did to get the pass. Was it a disciplinary
problem? She said no but that someone had made a racial
comment to her. I said to her this whole racial business about
being called black is a destruction of society. After all I told her
she was not black but brown. In America we have things all
screwed up when it comes to ethnicity. It seems that many
Americans think that anyone that has a tad of African in them is a
black. Few other countries actually take this concept to such an
extreme. Currently a man who many consider to be black has
become the President of the United States in 2009. He is a very
brown man coming from the fertilization of a Caucasian woman

with an African man. The genes for making skin color are polygenetic meaning that a number of genes are involved. It just so happens that the genes coding for lots of melanin production dominate over the more fair-colored genes. Due to the polygenetic situation his inherited genes coded for a mildly brown coloration. Now we have already addressed why people come in colors but why are some specifically black or brown. It is all about melanin and it comes in three different molecular shapes. There exists eumelamin (DHI), eumelanin (DHICA), and pheomelanin. Pheomelanin tends to give humans red hair and reddish pigment. Those who have a high concentration of DHI have black skin and those possessing mostly DHICA have brown type coloration. Again those of the Caucasian persuasion just do not produce as much of either melanin types. It is all about the electromagnetic spectrum of the universe. This spectrum consists of all kinds of wavelengths of energy, which are traveling throughout the universe at the speed of light. The shorter the wavelength, the more energy with gamma rays being the strongest. As they go through the body in say a nuclear explosion they literally rip electrons from your cells and this is not good. Microwaves are also in the electromagnetic spectrum and they are constant throughout the universe. They are a residual affect from the Big Bang. We however are interested at this point in the visible light spectrum, which are the colors we see. Having slightly different wavelengths they make up the colors red, orange, yellow, green, blue, and violet. Leaves look green to us since they absorb all of the color wavelengths except green, which is reflected. The sky is blue since the blue wavelengths bounce off of the nitrogen molecules making up most of our atmosphere. So it is with our skin. When all of the colors of visible light strike one's eyeball then what we see is a white color. Therefore the skin of very white Caucasians reflects off all of the colors. Black is actually the absence of colors. People with black skin have high amounts of the eumelanin DHI and due to its molecular structure it absorbs all of the colors of visible light. When that happens our eyes see the color black. A brown colored human contains more of the eumelanin DHICA that absorbs most of the colors but reflects off some such as red and green. This causes the eyes to see brown and so there you have it. The new President is a red and green reflector! Now Africa of course has a rich history but most humans typically think most of the inhabitants are black. Actually 5 different groups inhabited this continent by 1,000 C.E. They are somewhat loosely classified as blacks, whites, African Pygmies, Khoisan, and Asian. Blacks have in general occupied the Southern Sahara region and the Sub-Saharan region. Whites although light brown in color were to be found in Egypt, Libya, and Morocco. The Pygmies of which about 200,000 now exist actually differ from the blacks. They of course are smaller but have more reddish and less black skin. They possess more body hair and have a more prominent forehead, eyes, and teeth. They have lived for years in the central forests and currently live by many black farmers. Few people have actually heard of the Khoisan that sometimes are referred to as bushmen. Their skin takes on a yellowish tint and the females tend to accumulate much fat in their buttocks. This is scientifically known as steatopygia for whatever that is worth. They live in southern areas of Africa although Europeans as well as other Africans wiped out most of them. Many did interbreed with Europeans to become the coloreds of South Africa. Having an Asian group of people in 1,000 C.E. is interesting and they settled on the big island of Madagascar. Today the language there is Austronesian. It is possible they came by boat from India or South East Asia but some feel they actually made it the long way directly from Borneo. That would have simply been an amazing feat. Africa actually is one of the most genetically diverse areas of the world. Migrations over thousands of years has led to a wide-ranging gene pool. The oldest group found there is the Hadzabe found in Tanzania. These are the original hunter-gathers who actually may never have left Africa. Although indigenous to eastern Africa they did migrate out in small groups and interbred with other groups. We know for example the pygmies and the Khoisan share many of the same specific genes found in the Hadzabe. Pygmies of course are diminutive people living in the dense forests. Actually the Hadzabe were rather short people until they mixed with taller Africans. The extreme short stature of the Pygmies is most likely caused by a continuous deficiency of vitamin D. Living in heavily shaded areas for thousands of years kept them from producing adequate amounts of this vitamin. Vitamin D is important in allowing calcium to enter the bones and as a result bone density and enlargement has been highly reduced. By far and away the most dominating group south of the Sahara is the Bantu group. This is actually a large group of black skinned Africans originally living in the western parts of Africa. They collectively spoke somewhat the same essential language. From about 5,000 B.C.E. they slowly worked there way east and south and spread their genes with people all over Africa south of the Sahara. Currently the term Bantu is a general label for over 400 ethnic groups in Africa. The Bantu's developed the concepts of agriculture, herding and metalworking and as they spread throughout Africa they took their skills with them. They developed many complex societies throughout all of Africa. Unfortunately of the 12 million slaves going to the "New World" most were of the Bantu group. This is the major reason some Americans call anyone with a hint of African in them black. Society needs to take a long hard look at itself and forget about labeling anyone with African genes black.

MUTUAL ASSURED DESTRUCTION

Once again Albert Einstein had lots of things figured out. He is well known for his famous equation $E = MC^2$. What this means is actually very easy to understand. We may think of it, as energy equals mass times the speed of light squared. That sort of is not easy to understand. It would be easier if we just said that 100% of a certain mass could be made into 100% energy. Of course he had to get real mathematical about the whole thing. So if we could take your body and make it into 100% energy what an explosion we would witness! So it is with uranium^{235}. This is the isotopic element that blew up Hiroshima at the end of World War II killing about 140,000 humans. The uranium was packed tightly in a ball about the size of a soft ball and when it went off it was equal to about 23,000 tons of TNT going off at one time. Its pretty neat to think that a softball amount of uranium could be made into 100% energy just like that! Well fortunately I guess that last statement is far from true. Actually only an exceeding small fraction of the uranium was made into energy. What happened to the rest of the mass? Well it was made into 2 new elements like barium and krypton. Neutrons were freed up in the explosion and so were huge amounts of harmful gamma rays. We have all seen mushroom clouds so it is apparent that even though only a fraction of the uranium was made into energy it was enough to do the job. If the uranium was made into 100% energy perhaps there goes Japan. Actually we are far from being able to do what Einstein said is possible. If we ever gain that ability what a power source we would have for peaceful usage. Hiroshima was the victim of the world's 2nd nuclear explosion with the first occurring on July 16, 1945 in Alamogordo, New Mexico. We first had to check out if the atomic fission bomb would work. Both actually worked so good that 3 days after Hiroshima we dropped a plutonium fission bomb on Nagasaki killing around 70,000 individuals. Yes these are humans we are talking about. Uranium^{235} and plutonium^{239} are the only two isotopic elements that can split (fission) in a nuclear reaction. Generally speaking a fission nuclear bomb contains a critical mass of either element and when neutrons are sent into the mass the elements split releasing energy, radiation, and 2 or 3 more neutrons per element. These neutrons then go and split more of the radioactive elements producing a chain reaction resulting in the nuclear explosion. Various other radioactive elements such as iodine^{131}, strontium^{90}, and other isotopes are produced in these reactions. The iodine can screw up one's thyroid and the strontium gets into our bones. Nuclear explosions are just not nice! One may survive the blast but get cancer later on in life. Now a nuclear fission explosion gets pretty hot. It can get as hot as 27,000,000 °F, which is what is found in the inner core of the sun. So around 1950 some American scientists got a light bulb to light up in their head. They knew of course that fusion occurs in the inner core of the sun. The sun once again is a big gaseous ball of hydrogen. At the high temperatures in the inner core hydrogen atoms are forced into each other forming helium and lots of heat energy is released. We know that on a warm day at the ocean. This is called nuclear fusion. So the scientists got it together and made the thermonuclear hydrogen bomb, which is pretty much the bomb of today. They packed a bomb with a critical mass of plutonium and then sort of filled the rest of the bomb with hydrogen. Of course this is highly simplified but that is the basic idea of the bomb. They set the bomb off in the Marshall Islands in 1952. To set if off an explosive charge sends neutrons into the plutonium creating a fission nuclear explosion. The heat of millions of degrees then instantaneously compresses the hydrogen and they then fuse into helium setting off a colossal explosion. The resulting explosion was 450 times more powerful than the bomb that destroyed Hiroshima. Unfortunately by 1953 the Soviet Union had exploded large thermonuclear fusion bombs. In 1961 they went nuts and actually exploded a huge one, which equaled 500,000 tons of TNT going off at one time. The nuclear arms race continued and both countries have developed all kinds of strange bombs. For example boosted fission bombs containing only a small amount of hydrogen have been produced. They give off massive amounts of radiation. We have also produced salted bombs where the outer core contains cobalt or gold. Upon detonation all kinds of radioactive isotopes are produced. If anything good came out of this it is that the United States and now Russia got into the concept of mutual assured destruction. Both sides since the 60's have had an arsenal of thousands of nuclear weapons. Artillery shells, missiles, torpedoes, cruise missiles, and even missiles from submarines can fire them. Both sides could totally obliterate each other so why bother. It is common knowledge that we used to park a sub deep in the Mediterranean Sea and one in the Sea of Japan loaded with missiles containing multi-nuclear warheads. If all of them had been fired, every major city in the Soviet Union would have been toast. Of course the

Soviet Union had all kinds of missiles to blast us to oblivion. So
it goes. Anyway other countries currently have nuclear weapons.
They include the United Kingdom, France, China, Israel, India,
Pakistan, and possibly North Korea. It was estimated in 2006
about 27,000 nuclear weapons were on the earth. Russia and the
United States have about 96% of them though both countries are
inactivating many of them. Israel has 100 or so and they can be
fired from Jericho missiles or by plane. Israel has been able to
produce nuclear weapons because they have a type of breeder
nuclear reactor. All of the other nuclear countries except Pakistan
also possess these reactors. The breeder reactor uses uranium^{238}
as its fuel. Uranium exists in our world as 3 isotopes, which
means they have differing numbers of neutrons. Uranium^{234}
makes up 0.0054% of our natural occurring uranium. Uranium^{235}
makes up 0.7204% and uranium^{238} makes up the remaining
99.2742%. Once again only uranium^{235}, which has 3 less neutrons
than uranium^{238}, is fissionable. The other uranium isotope is out
of the picture. There is however an interesting use for the
plentiful uranium^{238}. In the complicated breeder nuclear reactor
we can take it and readily convert it into plutonium^{239}, which does
fission. The world has made about 1,200 metric tons of the stuff
of which 260 tons have been produced for weapons. The rest has
been used for generating electricity and is not weapons grade. So
again those nuclear countries having those reactors fill their
bombs with plutonium and hydrogen. That is not the case for
Pakistan. They have had to use uranium^{235} for their bombs and it
is very difficult to get enough of the purified stuff to make a
fission weapon. That was one of the big problems during World
War II when we did the Manhattan Project. This of course was
one of the most complicated tasks in history and we partially owe
it to Albert Einstein. He was not a part of the project but he did
send a letter to President Roosevelt warning him that German
nuclear scientists may ultimately have the capability of making a
fission bomb. This started the Manhattan Project, which produced
the world's most damaging weapon. The big problem though was
how to separate minute quantities of uranium^{235} from the plentiful

uranium^{238}. So what we did was get a bunch of uranium from the Congo and we built thousands of centrifuges that have microscopic pores. The uranium was made into a powder and was reacted with fluoride gas. This mixture was then sent through the thousands of centrifuges with each having slightly smaller sizes. Because uranium^{238} has 3 more neutrons than uranium^{235} it has a slightly higher mass. By the time the uranium-fluoride gas got through the last of the centrifuges only uranium^{235} made it through the microscopic holes. We got enough for a couple of critical masses and were able to bomb Japan. So it is with Pakistan and they have a small number of fission bombs. But here is a potential kicker. Nuclear scientists from Pakistan have given some of this technology to Iran and many in the world believe they will make nuclear weapons. We presently know they have a number of centrifuges but they say they are only for purifying uranium to make electricity. Many in the United States and Israel think otherwise and worry that a nuclear Iran will only goof up the Middle East even more. If they got fission bombs would they possibly nuke Israel? One answer to that is that Jerusalem is one of Islam's religious cities. My personal perspective on that is that nuking that city would be out of the question. But what about a fission bomb on the capital Tel Aviv? Well it is only 34 miles from the ancient city so who knows? Israel has a very good missile system and could easily send over 20 or 30 thermonuclear bombs to Iran. What will happen in this scenario is anybodies guess. Iraq had just about built a nuclear reactor by 1981and had vowed to destroy Israel. So the Israelis decided to take matters into their own hands. Eight pilots took new F-16 fighter jets and flew under radar for over 620 miles to Baghdad and destroyed the plant never to be rebuilt. But that was many years ago and Iran has good defenses. It would be much harder to destroy their nuclear facilities but certainly could be done. Israel also possesses a huge nuclear deterrent which I am sure Iran has some feelings about. We can only hope for peace to come to the Middle East. We should also hope that one of these years peace would descend upon the whole world. The likelihood of that however is but a pipe dream. Radical extremists are most certainly trying to acquire plutonium for a small fission bomb. They are also seeking the complex equations need to fire all needed mechanisms. They most likely will get enough weapons grade plutonium and the world must be aware of the horrid potentials. In time they could even get enough pure uranium^{235} from a country like Iran. Even the potential from a dirty bomb could cause mayhem in some part of the world. The dirty bomb would use a plastic explosive containing nuclear radioisotopes that upon exploding would scatter radioactive particles around the area of the explosion. Many feel that the damage would be minimal since most likely the radioactive particles would come from stuff like radioactive hospital waste. It is true that would not be an extremely serious issue. However plutonium dust is the most poisonous substance on the earth. If it was packed into a dirty bomb and detonated in a big city we would have a big problem. Fortunately for now it is very dangerous to even be around the fine plutonium dust but in a complicated lab scenario such a devise could be produced. A savage mind exists for a small number of us humans and I fear the worst is not over.

LIONS DO NOT MAKE VITAMIN D

Humans as already mentioned are able to synthesize vitamin D when they are exposed to ultra violet B rays zooming into us from the sun. We used to think this vitamin was pretty much only used by us to help get dietary calcium and phosphorous into our bloodstream. Well that is certainly true but now we know it is really needed in the body for many other extremely important functions. Recent information for example is showing that it may not only prevent cancer but also help cancer victims to survive. Cancer of course is a major issue for humans and in the United States approximately 1 out of every 3 humans will get it. A big reason for that is that we are just living longer. However we are also taking into our bodies more poisonous chemicals (free radicals) than anytime in history. Some humans also have inherited some shaky genes that increase their risk of getting certain cancers. Cancer is a total malfunction of the wiring in our

DNA. All of our cells contain regulatory genes (proto-oncogenes) that regulate how often our cells divide. Different types of regulatory genes exist. Most of the time cells are just busy doing their business and certain genes keep those cells working as needed. Sometimes specific proteins come into the cell telling it to go into cell division and make 2 more of the same cells. At this time other regulatory genes are turned on and they tell the cell to go into programmed cell division. When the 2 new cells are being produced other regulatory genes are turned on and the proteins they produce make sure the new strands of DNA are in perfect shape. If the new DNA is not in perfect shape other regulatory genes turn on and tell these new cells to go into programmed cellular death (apoptosis). This can happen quite frequently since cell division is a complex process. Unfortunately sometimes our regulatory genes go bad and the cell loses its ability to control itself. Regulatory genes may go bad for a number of reasons but it is often due to damage from free radicals. Free radicals constantly damage our DNA by ripping electrons from the DNA. Fortunately we all have DNA repairing genes but sometimes they receive too much free radical damage. When this happens and the DNA is not repaired and if the damage is to regulatory genes the cell may go bonkers. Different genes get turned on and the cell starts to make all kinds of proteins that cause the cell to become cancerous. These new proteins activate all kinds of new pathways, which is not good. They cause the cells to keep on dividing at very fast rates. They cause the cell to produce proteins that leave the cell and tell the surrounding area to produce more blood vessels. These new blood vessels will feed lots of nutrients to the overgrowing cells. New proteins are produced which leave the cell and destroy good cells. New proteins are produced that alter our immune system making it difficult for us to kill the cancer cells. Obviously losing our regulatory genes causes massive problems. In many cases the cancer cells break away from their original area and go into the bones, liver, lymph, and even the brain. Of course when that happens the results need not be discussed. So what are we to do? Well the obvious answer is to avoid free radicals (quit smoking) and take in optimal amounts of antioxidants. We should also make sure we get in an optimal amount of sunlight so we produce lots of vitamin D. This vitamin is very important in regulating many of our genes. This is especially true of the proto-oncogenes and the genes involved in normal cell growth. More specific information is needed but we do know more people get cancer that live in the northern hemisphere than who live in sunny climates. We also know that more cancer victims survive in sunny climates. A new Canadian study has shown that breast cancer victims having low levels of vitamin D do not survive as well as those having optimal levels. So all in all having optimal levels of this vitamin is very important. It is also needed to boost up our immune system, which fights infections. Up north low levels of it in the winter is one of the reasons we get sick. Having optimal levels of it allows our skin cells to produce loads of antimicrobial peptides that are a first line of defense against viruses and bacteria. These peptides blast into the foreign agents and actually create a hole in them that kills them. These include bacteria from open wounds and even flu viruses trying to get into our respiratory tract. Optimal vitamin D levels activate our white blood cells so that they can rapidly get to areas of infections. It also helps them to fight the infection at a faster rate. Vitamin D also causes us to rapidly produce antibodies that destroy infections and it also causes us to produce the proper amount of inflammatory molecules that also fight infections. Now of course many authorities are saying we should stay away from the sun, which is just ridiculous in most cases. Yes it is true skin cancer rates are rising and those highly susceptible should be very careful. But skin cancer is a funny scenario in general. Each year in the United States about 800,000 humans get basal cell carcinoma. It however almost never leaves the skin and goes to other areas of the body. Just burn it off the skin and one is good to go. About 200,000 humans get squamous cell carcinoma and it is just like its basal cell relative. We do have to watch out for malignant melonoma since it can rapidly go into the body. It causes about 1.5% of the cancer deaths in the United

States on a yearly basis. It has somewhat of a genetic basis in some people but most get it from too many sunburns throughout a lifetime. Fortunately the superficial type is the most common and it tends to travel across the skin from the initial site before penetrating deeper in the body. If caught early it is highly treatable. So all in all having optimal levels of vitamin D protects us from cancer and reduces infections. So what we should do is just get naked and go out into the sun for about 20 minutes per day and many of us can make up to 20,000 IUs of vitamin D per day. If the naked thing is not for you just go out with some dress and stay out longer. If you have dark skin or are over 60 years of age you have to stay out even longer. Just protect vulnerable areas and you should be fine. If you live in the dreary north during winter head to the local store and take in on a daily basis 2,000 IUs of vitamin D_3. It is the best form used by the body. Lots of other animals like horses, pigs, cows, sheep, and rats produce their own vitamin D from the sun. Even some fish, amphibians, reptiles, and some birds can produce it. All animals are different in their vitamin D requirements and this is an evolutionary adaptation in them all. A lion for example does not have the ability to produce vitamin D. It gets enough of it by eating other animals, which contain it in their body parts. Your cat and dog also cannot produce vitamin D. We know that since we have experimentally taken off the fur from these two characters and exposed them to the sun. They still did not produce it. If one wants to know the biochemistry, dogs and cats produce too much of the enzyme 7-dehydrocholesterol reductase. This enzyme keeps vitamin D from being made in the skin. But do not worry about your precious pets. Dogs and cats have eaten all kinds of animals for years and so they have been able to keep up with their vitamin D requirements. Dog and cat food is also fortified with the stuff. But be careful with other pets. For example feeding parrots and things like iguanas too much vitamin D can destroy their kidneys. Nature knows what is best and the critters of the world have once again evolutionary wise got it together.

DIMETHYL SULFOXIDE

If you cannot make money on something then perhaps you should say it does not work. Such may be the case with the solvent dimethyl sulfoxide (DMSO). As a by-product from the wood industry it has been used as a solvent since 1953. In 1961 Dr. Stanley Jacob was the head of the organ transplant program at Oregon Health Sciences University. He was messing with some DMSO figuring out if it could preserve organs. He soon found out that it can easily penetrate human skin and so he really started to study it. He found out it can relieve pain, reduce inflammation, and promote healing. Before you know it a bunch of pharmaceutical companies started to study its potential values. Clinical studies were performed but in 1965 an Irish women died of some type of allergic reaction while taking DMSO along with several other drugs. The DMSO was not found to be the cause of death. Then came along a study that showed that dogs, rabbits, and pigs receiving huge amounts of DMSO had lens changes to their eyes. So the FDA halted all further studies on DMSO. Of interest is that studies in other parts of the world have found absolutely no lens changes from DMSO application in humans or other primates. The drug companies did not really get upset about further studies on DMSO for a couple of reasons. One of the reasons is that when you apply it to the skin it soon makes your sweat smell like garlic for a while. That may make it hard to market even though that it is quite harmless. Furthermore it is extremely cheap to buy and they sure do not like that. A final kicker to them is that no company could actually patent it so they just quit paying attention to it. That is basically only in the United States. Other countries tended to follow studies performed on DMSO from around the world. Over 40,000 articles about its chemistry have been written in scientific articles. Medical articles have been written and they number over 11,000. A lot is known about DMSO and it is considered to be extremely safe when taken either internally or externally. It is currently approved for use medicinally in 125 countries and it is one of the vet's major medicines. The FDA approved it for musculoskeletal use on horses and dogs in 1970. They routinely apply it to the sore muscles of horses and also for arthritic conditions. It is perfectly legal to purchase DMSO and it is available at local health food stores. It comes somewhat diluted in a 70% formula, which is good since this is the best absorbed into the body. So what is it good for as far as humans are concerned? Well first of all DMSO readily penetrates our tissues because it is polar and it is a very small molecule. It easily goes through cell membranes and is able to intermix with the water molecules making up most of the parts of our cells. As a result it can penetrate throughout the entire cell where it can do its job. One of these is to relieve pain and promote healing of tissue. Pain is reduced because the DMSO goes into the peripheral nerve C pain fibers and inactivates them. How DMSO promotes the healing of wounds and burns is somewhat more complicated. DMSO has been shown to stabilize cell membranes that may be damaged due to trauma. It is a very potent antioxidant, which is able to neutralize the strongest free radicals. Trauma to cells results in a tremendous burst of superoxide free radicals and the most damaging of all, which is known as the hydroxyl free radical. Through electron donation DMSO neutralizes these radicals reducing damage and allows the cell to better repair itself. It also relaxes blood vessels so that more nutrients can get to the site of the injury. Of added interest is that DMSO promotes the healing of new tissue and halts scar tissue growth. DMSO is also great at stopping inflammation itself mostly through its antioxidant abilities. To really get a good affect add it to a hydrocortisone cream and the hydrocortisone will get to the site of the inflammation much faster. It is great for sore muscles and sprains. This sort of brings us to arthritis that so many people suffer from to some degree. Arthritis is all about pain and inflammation and DMSO has been shown to reduce the pain and inflammation when applied often to swollen joints. Some doctors are even giving it in injection form to the site of injury with great results. Being highly nontoxic humans have been given very high doses for up to 30 days without any major problems. Some people get headaches when it is injected and all will smell like garlic for days but both conditions go away. It has been found to not harm the immune system, circulatory system, and even the liver and kidneys. It has been FDA approved for reducing the inflammation caused to the bladder from interstitial cystitis and those receiving it get many injections of it. What is really interesting is that it might hold promise for stroke victims and those who suffer from a closed internal head injury. DMSO has been given internally to stroke victims whose stroke is caused by a blood clot. The DMSO has been found to get to the area of the stroke and reduce both inflammation and damage to the brain cells. It has been shown to especially work well if fructose sugar is also injected in the solution. The fructose allows the damaged brain cells to make quick energy for repair purposes. Hopefully some of the more open-minded countries in the world will take the lead in the internal uses of this substance. But for now its also great for a sore lower back. Just remember though that many of us are allergic to certain chemicals and this could be true of DMSO. So the first time you apply it just use a small amount and see what happens. If nothing happens use it at will but remember you might just smell like garlic for a while.

BRAIN OF THE CENTURY

So many books have been written about Albert Einstein that it would be foolish to do a biographical thought. Suffice it to say that it is amazing that 100 years after he started to put forth his theories most still survive intact. Computers of today are amazing and yet he just used a pencil and paper to describe the universe. If he was around today the world would just go bonkers with what he could now accomplish. But alas it is not to be. Therefore some quotes from this guy just may be of order. "It has been mentioned that according to the general theory of relativity, a ray of light will experience a curvature of its path when passing through a gravitational field, this curvature being similar to that experienced by the path of a body which is projected through a gravitational field. As a result of this theory, we should expect that a ray of light which is passing close to a heavenly body would be deviated toward the latter. For a ray of light which passes the sun at a distance of Δ sun-radii from its center, the angle of deflection (a) should amount to a = 1.7 seconds of arc/ Δ." This was indeed confirmed by photographs taken of the solar eclipse of May 29, 1919, which made him super famous. Here are some more quotes not in any logical order. "I never failed in mathematics before I was fifteen. I had mastered differential and integral calculus." "The religious inclination lies in the dim consciousness that dwells in humans that all nature, including the humans in it, is in no way an accidental game, but a work of lawfulness, that there is a fundamental cause of all existence." "Do not worry about your difficulties in Mathematics. I can assure you mine are still greater." "Science without religion is lame. Religion without science is blind." "Reality is merely an illusion, albeit a persistent one." "Two things are infinite: the universe and human stupidity; and I am not sure about the universe." I know not with what weapons World War III will be fought, but World War IV will be fought with sticks and stones." "Great spirits have often encountered violent opposition from mediocre minds." "We can't solve problems by using the same kind of thinking we used when we created them." "My religion consists of a humble admiration of the illimitable superior spirit who reveals himself in the slight details we are able to perceive with our frail and weak minds." "The further the spiritual evolution of mankind advances, the more certain it seems to me that the path to genuine religiosity does not lie through the fear of life, and the fear of death, and blind faith, but through striving after rational knowledge." "Every one who is seriously involved in the pursuit of science becomes convinced that a spirit is manifest in the laws of the Universe – a spirit vastly superior to that of man, and in one in the face of which we with our modest powers must feel humble. In this way the pursuit of science leads to a religious feeling of a special sort, which is indeed quite different from the religiosity of someone more naïve." "What is the meaning of human life, or, for that matter, of the life of any creature? To know an answer to this question means to be religious. You ask: Does it make any sense, then, to pose this question? I answer: The man who regards his own life and that of his fellow creatures as meaningless is not merely unhappy but hardly fit for life." "Denominational traditions I can only consider historically and psychologically; they have no other significance to me." "If we are to have in the universe an average density of matter which differs from zero, however small may be that difference, then the universe cannot be quasi-Euclidean. On the contrary, the results of calculation indicate that if matter be distributed uniformly, the universe would necessarily be spherical (or elliptical). Since in reality the detailed distribution of matter is not uniform, the real universe will deviate in individual parts from the spherical, *i.e.* the universe will be quasi-spherical. But it will be necessarily finite. In fact, the theory (General Theory of Reality) supplies us with a simple connection between the space-expanse of the universe and the average density of matter in it." Albert Einstein died on Monday, April 18, 1955 of a burst aortic aneurysm. He was 76 years old. Shortly before his death he was very sick but busy jotting down more mathematical equations.

ANOTHER BIG COMET

It is now commonly contended that a huge comet or asteroid blasted into the earth near the Yucatan Peninsula roughly 65 million years ago and wiped out the dinosaurs and countless other living specimens. Throughout the earth an unusual layer of earth high in the element iridium is found at this time period. Iridium is a most unusual element found in only small amounts on earth. However it is plentiful in asteroids and comets. Catastrophic events have occurred many times throughout our earth's history including one that may have occurred only 12,900 years ago. Our earth was just getting over the last major ice age and people were in motion. Asiatic people had come to North America around 14,000 years ago and by 12,900 years ago had spread east and south from the Bering Strait. Up near the Great Lakes were groups of now called Native Indians. They were called the Clovis people due to the type of sharp fluted arrowheads they used. These arrowheads were originally dug up in Clovis, New Mexico. For a thousand years these natives hunted and gathered and hung around a very strange bunch of giant mammals. Currently known as megafauna, these were the giant mammals like the wholly mammoth and the sabre-toothed cat. Giant ground sloth's were roaming around that weighed over 5 tons along with the Giant Ice Age Bison. It had horns that spanned over 7 feet. An 8 foot long American lion was around along with a giant beaver that was also over 8 feet long. The nastiest critter was the short-faced bear that when standing stood over 11 feet tall. Actually over 145 other species of giant animals roamed around North America and others were found all over the world. All had been around for millions of years along with their smaller family members. The Clovis people certainly hunted some of them and some humans were probably also devoured by the huge carnivores. They seemed to prefer the wholly mammoth since their village sites contain many of their bones. We have even pulled mammoth bones out of deep glacial lakes in Pennsylvania, which have crude ropes, attached to them. That was probably an early form of meat preservation. But anyway around 12,900 years ago the Clovis people were gone and most of the giant mammals disappeared at the same time. This brings us to the concept of comets. We have all heard of them but what are they all about? Well they are enormous balls of ice and dust. They are considered to be "icy dirtballs" or "dirty iceballs" according to their rough characteristics. However very roughly speaking they tend to somewhat contain the same masses of ice and dirt. The dirt is the most interesting part of the comet from a scientific point since we now know most of the chemicals contained in the dust. The vast majority of the compounds are carbon based but silicon compounds also exist. The carbon compounds go from very simple ones like carbon monoxide and carbon dioxide to more complex ones like polyaromatic hydrocarbons. Some of the carbon-containing substances contain hydrogen, oxygen, and nitrogen. Other strange carbon substances include formaldehyde, methanol, and acetylene. Comets even contain hydrogen cyanide, ammonia, and hydrogen sulfide. We shall soon see it is the vast number of carbon compounds that provide evidence to the destruction of the Clovis people and megafauna. Comets have passed by earth for billions of years and many have blasted into our atmosphere. Most likely trillions of comets exist and in our solar system they are to be found in the Oort Cloud, and the Kuiper belt with its associated scattered discs. We believe the Oort Cloud is located about 1 light year from our sun with the Kuiper belt being closer. These areas contain the comets that were produced at the same time as our solar system. The Oort Cloud is approximately 5 times the mass of earth and was produced as matter got close to the gravitational masses of Jupiter and was ejected outwards into long elliptic orbits. What causes some of these comets to leave their orbits and be projected toward our sun is still somewhat theoretical. Many scientists believe that the Milky Way itself contains tidal forces that bends and distorts various bodies in our outer Solar System. At times this bending causes comets to leave their usual orbits. Scientists also believe the Oort Cloud and the Kuiper belt is also affected by the gravitational pull from near-by stars or even giant molecular clouds. Whatever the reason comets on occasion leave the Cloud or Kuiper belt and come in proximity of our sun and planets. Of course it is well known that as it gets closer to the sun it begins to melt and the volatile gases heat up forming the well-known tail of the comet. Some comets are very interesting in that they periodically go by the earth in their long orbital patterns. Long-period comets initially come from the Oort Cloud and may take thousands of years to make their loop by the earth. Short-period comets usually come from the Kuiper belt area and may loop by in less than 200 years. Of interest is that the well-known Halley's Comet, which loops every 75 – 76 years originated from the Oort Cloud. Last seen in 1986 it will be back in 2061. Unfortunately its appearance in 1986 was the worst for observing for thousands of years. But that may have not been true for the Clovis people 12,900 years ago. They may have possibly slowly witnessed a comet coming right at them and exploding over what is now eastern Canada. If that is true then there would have been a massive explosion killing off plants, animals, and even humans in a very large area. Fires would have been extreme and long lasting. Devastation would have occurred for thousands of square miles and total upheaval of areas of our earth would have occurred. It is quite possible this event did occur and scientific evidence is now documenting the event. The evidence has presented itself from as far away as California and Belgium. The scientific evidence lies in a 12,900-year layer known as the "black mat". If you want to get geologic it is called the Younger Dryas event boundry because the world then went into a 1,000-year cold period known as the Younger Dryas cooling episode. When the black mat dirt is examined scientists have found high concentrations of iridium, extraterrestrial helium, charcoal, soot, carbon spherules, and glass-like carbon. The big kicker is that also found were tiny diamonds known as nanodiamonds. Nanodiamonds can only be formed from the intense heat and pressure, which an extra terrestrial object is subjected to when it hits our earth's atmosphere. The high amounts of soot and charcoal found would be due to the intense fires from the explosion. The nanodiamonds could only come from a carbon rich comet. So it is indeed possible that a comet led to the demise of the Clovis people and the megafauna of North America and even Europe. The intense fires could have lifted enough soot up into the air to change the climate. It is not necessarily true that all of the Clovis people and megafauna died at once. Most likely many survived in the southern extremes. But the damage may have been enough that the entire populations were radically altered leading their ultimate demise. Of course one may ask as to why animals such as deer, rabbits, squirrels, etc were able to survive. Well most likely there was a horrible destruction of most species but the survivors had better reproduction rates and were able to slowly recover. One may also ask why most of the other megafauna found throughout the world also disappeared over the time period humans were about. The answer to this may in certain areas have been climatic but humans caused most of the demise. Humans as they roamed the world became very efficient hunters and most of the megafauna were not like sabre-teeth tigers or the short-faced bear. One must remember human activity has occurred for thousands of years. But it is certainly interesting that a big comet might have been the big event of 12,900 years ago.

BOOZE

Thousands of years ago some early humans were busy pressing fruits into some sort of container. Why they did this is not known but probably was due too the fact that they learned how to make pottery. Maybe they decided to store some of the extra juice for a while or even just misplaced it. Anyway about a month later they decided to consume the juice. They drank a bunch of it and soon started to feel mentally different. They may have got somewhat euphoric and loud in speech. They may soon have got clumsy and bounced around for a while. Then they fell asleep. These humans had discovered ethyl alcohol (C_2H_5OH). They had just drunk yeast waste! Wild yeast are everywhere and we breathe them in with every breath we take. If they land on fruit they can be found on the skin of the fruit. These single celled fungi need to make energy from glucose sugar but their mechanism is different from plants and animals. They do not possess mitochondria so they can only breakdown glucose using a process called fermentation. When plants and animals make energy from glucose the waste products are carbon dioxide and water. Lots of energy is made from each glucose molecule. Yeast do not need to make much energy and when they breakdown glucose the waste products are carbon dioxide and ethyl alcohol. Fruits contain lots of glucose so when fruit juices are made wild yeast easily land on the juice. Fermentation soon starts and typically the yeast will keep making ethyl alcohol until all of the glucose is consumed. So throughout the last 8,000 years of human history all kinds of alcoholic drinks have been made mostly from using fruit as a base. Humans of course did also find that the starches found in grains could also be fermented to make various kinds of beers. They then found out that ethyl alcohol and water have different boiling temperatures so they could make a still and boil out and concentrate the alcohol. The Russians liked to use potatoes since starch is just millions of glucose molecules stuck together. Actually the production of alcoholic beverages helped save many of our early civilizations. In many societies the drinking water contained all kinds of viruses, bacteria, and nasty protozoans (protista). Drinking that water led to illnesses like cholera and dysentery. The alcoholic drinks were actually better to drink, as their pH was too low for many disease carrying bacteria or whatever. The alcohol also inhibited the growth of these species. Alcohol also was a brain chemical for us pleasure seeking humans. It is inherit to humans to feel good about our mind. Humans seek pleasure through all kinds of activities whether it be high risk behavior, meditation, overindulgence, etc. Some feel pleasure through skydiving, exotic foods, or mind-altering substances. Alcohol obviously affects the brain as a mind-altering substance. Shortly after consumption of ethyl alcohol this molecule goes through the blood brain barrier. In the brain the alcohol affects 3 major neurotransmitters. They are known as serotonin (5HT), gamma-aminobutyric acid (GABA), and dopamine. These neurotransmitters tend to either stimulate or inhibit various impulses in the brain. Serotonin is the major neurotransmitter in the brain in that it affects mood, thinking, emotions, and even motivation. It also helps to control appetite, sleep, learning, and even some hormones. Researchers found in the early 1980's that many people suffering from depression had low circulating levels of serotonin in the brain. It was being destroyed too rapidly by various brain neurons. So researchers developed prozac and other selective serotonin reuptake inhibitors which function to keep serotonin at optimal levels in the brain circulation. This has worked well for millions of individuals allowing them to much better enjoy life. Alcohol consumption increases the release of serotonin thereby altering many brain pathways. Moods may change along with many other normal thinking patterns. Alcohol also affects the release of GABA resulting in changes in memory patterns. Alcohol molecules in the brain also cause the release of dopamine that is our pleasure seeking neurotransmitter. Higher than normal levels of dopamine gives us somewhat of the happy feeling one gets from alcohol consumption. Nicotine from cigarettes also moderately releases dopamine in the brain and this is one reason addiction may occur. One of the interesting hormonal changes which occurs from alcohol consumption involves the change in the antidiuretic hormone (ADH). ADH causes our kidneys to reabsorb water back into the body's circulation. When one drinks, the alcohol confuses various osmoregulators in the hypothalamus of the brain. These osmoregulators regulate the overall pressure found in our body. Water of course is the major molecule involved with maintaining optimal pressures inside and outside of our cells. The alcohol tends to make the brain feel that too much pressure exists in the body. As a result the brain signals our pituitary gland, which secretes ADH into the body. The pituitary slows the production of ADH and as a result the kidneys start to excrete water into the bladder. Alcohol makes humans urinate a lot, which can actually lead to dehydration. So now one may ask what ultimately happens to the alcohol molecule so that humans do not always feel tipsy after consumption? Well typically males can breakdown about 1 ounce of alcohol per hour with females not being that efficient. Some is actually broken down in the stomach but most breakdown occurs in the liver. With the use of enzymes the ethyl alcohol is first made into toxic acetaldehyde. The acetaldehyde is made into acetic acid, which is really concentrated vinegar. Finally the acetic acid is made into carbon dioxide and water. Acetaldehyde unfortunately can be made into toxic free radicals so it is most important for anyone consuming alcohol to also consume antioxidants. In fact it has been shown that the consumption of antioxidants along with minerals and B vitamins negate damage to our body from acetaldehyde. Milk thistle supplements also neutralize the acetaldehyde and protect liver cells from injury. Anyone who consumes alcohol should also consume milk thistle. One should also certainly stay hydrated. Of additive interest is that alcoholic beverages contain other mind-altering chemicals other than ethyl alcohol. Let's take beer as an example. Traditional beer is made from barley, hops, yeast, and water. The barley is malted which is a process of just allowing the barley seeds to sit in water until they are just ready to germinate. Then the barley is roasted which allow enzymes to breakdown the starches into glucose molecules that can be readily fermented. Hops are added and this is a most unusual plant. Hops (*Humulus lupulus*) is the only other member of the family *Cannabaceae* which also includes marijuana (*Cannibus sativa*). Hops are just like marijuana in that it has male and female plants and it is the female flower that is added to make beer. Hop flowers contain many essential oils and the major chemical constituent is known as lupulin. Lupulin actually is an assortment of molecules and they possess sedative and even narcotic properties. Some of the chemicals act as a diuretic hence beer drinkers really urinate a lot! The lupulin complex also contains a molecule known as humulone. Of biochemical interest is that its molecular formula is $C_{21}H_{30}O_5$. This may be irrelevant to most people but the major active component in marijuana is known as THC. Its molecular formula is $C_{21}H_{30}O_2$. From a brain standpoint THC receptors may have a weak affinity for lupulin leading to THC derived alterations. Of final note hops also contain geraniol which has a formula of $C_{10}H_{17}OH$. Because of the OH group this is actually an alcohol molecule. So indeed beer drinking is not just about the ethyl alcohol (C_2H_5OH) molecule. That is also true about the consumption of various types of wines. Just about any kind of fruit can be used to make a good quality wine. Wine makers also use specific yeast known as *Saccharomyces cervisiae* that were originally found on oak trees to impart specific flavors to the wine. Through fermentation they of course produce the ethyl alcohol to be found in the wine. But other theoretical mind-altering substances are also made during the fermentation and aging process. Certain higher alcohols known as fusel oils are produced and they can make up to 50% of the total aromatics found in certain wines. They make it to the brain upon consumption. Examples of these include isobutyl alcohol and isoamyl alcohol that actually add fruitiness to the wine. It is also known that during the aging process that various types of tannins bind to some of the alcohol molecules. Little research has been done to examine their effects on the brain.

However, suffice it to say that wine drinkers feel different from the wine effects, as do beer consumers. So it is also with the consumption of spirits. All kinds of assorted molecules are also produced during the making of rums, whiskeys, etc. Many of these might also bind to ethyl alcohol and research into these substances needs to be better examined. But all in all the consumption of alcoholic beverages involves much more than just the ethyl alcohol molecules.

TWO UNITED STATES

Funny things can transpire when 70,000 soldiers end up fighting 100,000 soldiers and this is indeed true for the Battle of Gettysburg. Actually nothing was funny at all since there were over 51,000 casualties during this battle on July 1,2, and 3 in 1863. Over 10,000 were killed with 30,000 wounded. Well over 10,000 were either missing or captured after the battle. Somewhere around 21,000 men lay wounded in the fields for 2 or 3 days. Is it possible that the Confederates could have ultimately become its own nation if the Rebs would have won that battle? That of course is an unknown but it may have changed the tide and the North may have been ready for a peace treaty dividing our country in two. General Robert E. Lee with his 70,000-man army in the spring of 1863 moved north and ultimately made it to Pennsylvania. He was looking for food and supplies but mainly felt an attack towards Philadelphia may shake up the North. It may even be possible to swing around towards Washington and perhaps take the city. He was tired of the fight being fought on Southern soil. The Federal troops were more close to Washington but moved northwards slowly as the Confederates moved more up north. A north to south mountain ridge basically separated the 2 armies. Unfortunately for Lee his Calvary led by Major General J.E.B Stuart had left him and were roaming further north to see what trouble they could cause to the enemy. This hurt Lee since one of their jobs was to track the Federal armies position. They only played a small part on the final day of battle. Anyway, the Rebs passed through the Cashtown Mountain pass and came to Gettysburg. The Feds moved northwest from around Washington and came to Gettysburg. Gettysburg had some nice hills around it and both armies wanted to be on the top of the hills for good field position. Seminary Ridge being closer to Gettysburg was nice but the better position was Cemetery Ridge. The battle began on the morning of July 1st and swung back and forth as such. By 4:15 pm the Feds left Seminary Ridge and retreated back to Cemetery Ridge offering a good position for the next day. Lee might have been able to drive them from Cemetery Ridge by first taking a place called Culps Hill. He sent a courier to Lt. General Richard Ewell to attack "if practical". However Ewell knew his troops were tired and he was in lots of pain from an "infected stump" from a previous battle. He decided to wait for another division to arrive before trying to take the hill. They did arrive around dusk but by then the Feds had more men in the area and things just did not work out for the Rebs. Did the world order possibly change partly due to an "infected stump"? So anyway some people got to sleep that night and the morning came with the hot sun coming up. Many more troops slowly came into their positions. The Feds had a 3-mile long line with one end being at the famous Little Round Top. For various reasons the days battle did not start until 4 pm. Little Round Top was actually not occupied at that time and could easily been taken by the Rebs. This could have been the start of a flanking of the Federal position allowing the Rebs to get around the Feds. But it was not to be since they did not go after this position early and ultimately the 20th Maine under Colonel Joshua Chamberlain arrived and occupied Little Round Top. As the gigantic battle raged all over the place the rebel Alabamians fought to get up Little Round Top under fierce fire from the 20th Maine. Chamberlain's soldiers became low on ammunition and it looked as if the Rebs would win and a flanking maneuver could be commenced. However Chamberlain told his depleted forces to "fix bayonets" and charge the Rebs. They did and the Rebs fled and Little Round Top was saved. Is it possible that if the charge did not occur and that the 20th did not fight as hard that a flanking would have occurred? If so could have the Rebs got around the Feds in force creating a winning scene? Nobody knows the

answer to this but Chamberlain most certainly became an America
hero after this battle. Anyway by the end of the second day the
Rebs really did not gain much ground and the Feds were still
entrenched on Cemetery Ridge. On the third and final day Lee
decided that a massive bombardment with 140 cannons directly in
the center of the Feds position would soften them up and 13,000
brave souls could then attack this area. All they had to do was
walk up a hill for hundreds of yards and blast away at the
remaining Feds hiding behind a stonewall! Major General George
Pickett's newly arrived division would be the major actors in the
charge. The cannon fire started in the early afternoon with 140
Reb cannons blasting the Fed line for one and one/half hours. The
60 Federal cannon fired back but mostly held back until the
charge. Unfortunately a funny thing happened for the Rebs. Most
of their cannon fire overshot their targets and the damage inflicted
was minor in the long run. When the firing ceased 13,000 Rebs
trucked up through the field and the Feds pored artillery with
shrapnel and canister down on the walking soldiers. By the way
each canister contained 25 1-inch balls packed in tin cylinders.
The carnage can only be imagined! The Rebs kept coming and
some actually came close to the stonewall only to be met with
rifle fire from the protected Feds. The Rebs had little chance and
retreat was the way to go. Confederate losses exceeded 50% and
some regiments had 85% casualties. The battle was over but the
war continued for a couple more years. One unusual man who
fought in the battle was the famous John Burns. He was in the
War of 1812 but most likely saw little action. He had said that he
fought in the Second Seminole War and the Mexican War but no
evidence indicates this to be true. But he did indeed fight at
Gettysburg and he was over 70 years old. On the first day of
battle this man from Gettysburg went up to the 150th
Pennsylvanian Infantry wearing: "dark trousers and waist coat, a
blue "swallow tail" coat with burnished brass buttons, such as
used to be affected by well-to-do gentlemen of the old school
about forty years ago, and a high black silk hat". He had with him
an antique Enfield rifle. He wanted to fight the Rebs and was

accepted but told to go to a fairly safe area in the woods. He was soon given a more modern rifle by a member of the 7th Wisconsin. It is quite possible that he then moved up with a skirmish line and shot 2 – 4 Rebs including an officer on a horse. However as time moved on and the Rebs were advancing he was wounded 3 - 5 times and retreated but he had to lie down. Burns said of his last wound:"Down I went, and the whole Rebel Army ran over me". He was wounded severely in the left leg and the other 2 were rather minor. He did have the presence to throw away his gun and bury his remaining cartridges so the Rebs would think he was just an innocent victim. Sometimes it is good to be an old man! It then appears that he lay in the field all night. It also appears that he was finally taken into town in a wagon as he was considered to be just a citizen. He survived his wounds and became a famous figure of the Gettysburg campaign. Unfortunately for thousands of other fighters their ordeal was just getting started. If you were wounded in the chest, stomach, or groin typically you might be just left in the field to die. Physicians did not know why but even if the bullet was removed you usually expired within a couple of days. Today we know that a sucking wound brings with it all kinds of battle dust containing gas gangrene bacteria (*Clostridium perfringens*). These anaerobic bacteria exists as a spore in soil and when it gets into a wound that clots, it starts to grow producing poisons that destroy tissue. The result is typically a nasty death. So those poor souls were mostly left to die. If you got shot in the arms or legs it was your lucky day. You would end up in some field hospital and just undergo a real nice bloody, unsterilized amputation. A typical amputation of the arm might go something like this. The wounded soldier would hopefully receive some whiskey and opium pills. Lying on a slab he would be given chloroform if available and a tourniquet was applied towards the shoulder. Using a long Catling Amputation knife the surgeon would cut through the center of the arm midway between the elbow and shoulder. A flap of tissue was then cut from inside out on the front of the upper arm and the back of the upper arm. The surgeon would then pull the skin up the arm. A saw would then slice through the bone severing the arm, which was usually thrown into a pile. Arteries and veins would be squeezed tight near the amputation with silk thread. The tourniquet was loosened and any bleeding was stopped and blood clots removed. The skin flaps would then be sutured covering the bone at the place of amputation. Dressings were applied and a bandage roll covered the stump and upper arm. The soldier was then carried to a place to lie down. Ultimately the thousands of amputees stayed in hospital tents for weeks and would hopefully survive. They often had fevers and their stumps would become swollen and inflamed. Pus would often have to be drained and all in all it was a very bad time. But for many healing occurred but the war was over for these guys. Sometimes it is just very nice to live in modern times!

THE OCEANS

Currently around one-half of our world's populations live in the coastal areas surrounding our oceans. At the present rate of growth the numbers are going to just continue to climb. Fish consumption has doubled in the last 25 years to more than 90 million tons. That may be fine and dandy from a health perspective but the oceans are in peril. Pollution, climate change, and over fishing are rapidly changing the scope of our vast oceans. All of the oceans are being over stressed and of course humans are the culprits. Take oxygen levels as an example. The oceans are warming and cold-water holds more dissolved oxygen than does warm water. The reason for this is quite simple. In warm water the oxygen molecules bounce off of each other and other molecules at a faster pace and so tend to pass out faster into the atmosphere. We are also sending into the oceans huge amounts of nitrogen and phosphorous from agricultural runoff and sewage. These nutrients cause algae to grow like mad and then die off in huge amounts. When they sink towards the bottom bacteria break them down using up even more oxygen. This is the well-known event called eutrophication and it is also affecting vast bays like the Chesapeake. It appears now that the oceans are not absorbing as much carbon dioxide as they used to do. Approximately one-half the amount of carbon dioxide is being absorbed as was in the mid 1990s. It is possible that the oceans have become saturated with the stuff. It may also be somewhat due to changes in the surface waters due to overall changes in weather cycles. If this is really true then we really must slow down carbon dioxide production on a world scale to counter global warming. It is also well known that our glaciers are melting especially in the Artic and the Greenland Ice Sheet. This ice sheet has a volume of about 2.9 million cubic kilometers and when gone will not come back for many generations. The effect on our coastlines from this melting may ultimately be catastrophic. From a European perspective the melting of this cold water from the ice sheet may affect the easterly Golf Stream resulting in a colder Western Europe. Coastal areas such as Florida and Bangladesh, which are near sea level, might not be around if things continue as they are today. It might be wise to look further into the potential problems Florida may encounter. For example in 2005 the Gulf of Mexico had their worst red tide explosion in 34 years. Excessive nutrients may have been partly the culprit and the red tide killed millions of pounds of fish. Also killed were manatees, dolphins, and sea turtles. The Florida tidal shore goes for 8,426 miles with 825 miles of sandy beaches. People are moving there in droves! In the 1940's the population was 2 million but now it is 13 million. It is projected that the population will be 26 million by 2030 and it is already loaded with oceanic problems. There are 62 Superfund pollution sites along Florida's gulf. Radioactive and nutrient-filled wastewater sits in giant pits polluting the waters. Between 3 – 4 million sewage plants and septic tanks leak nutrient rich wastewaters into the rivers and the ocean. Mercury consumption advisories occur on a daily basis. The ever-growing cruise ship industry is also causing pollution headaches and is not well regulated. For example in 1 week a typical cruise ship generates 210,000 gallons of sewage, 1 million gallons of gray water, 37,000 gallons of oily bilge water, 8 tons of solid waste, and millions of gallons of ballast water. Most of this stuff can be dumped 3 miles off of shore. Many people think that offshore oil wells are non-polluting because we just worry about oil spills that seldom occur. However drilling operations give off an average of 180,000 gallons of waste muds and cuttings per well. Also "produced water" which is water brought up from a well with oil and gas is also a problem. Each drilling platform discharges hundreds of thousands of gallons of this stuff every day and it is loaded with benzene, arsenic, lead, zinc, naphthalene, and toluene. The costs of the pollutants, along with global change, are staggering. Between 1996 and 2001 the Keys have experienced a 40% decrease in coral covering. Global warming certainly may be factored into this problem. The fishing industry is also being highly affected. Every year recreational fisherman harvest 187 million fish with 90 million captured and released. Many of the released do not live very long after being hooked. Commercial fishing in 2004 harvested 110 million pounds of marine life and this cannot be sustained. They also with their fishing techniques get rid of all kinds of so-called "bycatch" which are the living organisms not worth keeping but make up a huge part of the overall ecosystem. This typically consists of 20 – 30% of what they catch and is a worldwide problem. All of this cannot continue since the stocks of fish are rapidly dwindling and we are just talking about Florida. In many parts of the ocean the over fishing is even worse. It is estimated that one-third of our commercial stocks have collapsed and by 2050 all commercial stocks will be gone. Currently only 6 of the 26 species commercially hunted in the 1960's remain in commercial quantities. Overall species are declining near the shores as the huge human population is taking them for individual food sources throughout the world. We have vast commercial fleets that are actually subsidized by their governments to keep the fleets profitable. These governments fork out 20 billion dollars a year in subsidies so that the commercial fleets can buy bait, fuel, and ice or otherwise they would shut down. This must be stopped but it is an 80 – 100 billion-dollar industry and humans tend to not think about the future. All in all things look quite dismal but if the world responds perhaps in years stocks may rebound. But economically now many countries are looking at making huge fish farms located up to 200 miles offshore. This may help in the near future and may unfortunately be one of the only answers. The future is once again quite grim. The coral reefs around the world are undergoing rapid and severe bleaching that may be partly due to global warming and excessive UV light from ozone depletion. Pollution however is also actively involved since these reefs have a very fragile ecosystem. Even water temperature changes may affect the coral. Bleaching is when the coral turn white which is a sign of death. Coral are in the phylum *Cnidaria* and are related to jellyfish. Millions of these small polyps exist on a reef that they actually make from the calcium carbonate molecules found in huge amounts in the oceans. They possess small stinging nematocysts (tentacles) that function to capture small organisms. But most of them are also coated with a single-celled algae known as *Zoogloanthellae*. These algae remove carbon dioxide and nitrogen wastes from the coral allowing them to live in dense concentrations. The algae get a nice place to live and lots of carbon dioxide for photosynthesis. These algae also give coral reefs their color. Unfortunately the changes being experienced by the oceans are killing the *Zoogloanthellae* and although they can come back in many cases the damage is too severe. When these algae die the delicate balance of the coral may be destroyed and the coral themselves die off. The reef will then be totally altered in a bad way. It is unknown whether coral bleaching may be halted at this time. Finally it should be noted that perhaps the most delicious tasting crab in the world is in serious peril. For those in the "know" the Chesapeake Bay Blue Crab (*Callinectes sapidus*) is the ultimate in taste. Found mostly throughout the coastal areas of Maryland and Virginia it has a long history in these areas. Unfortunately in the last 15 years it has experienced a 70% decline in its population. Perhaps it best sums up the problems of the ocean. Too many people over harvesting this delicacy along with changes in the water chemistry caused by pollution, temperature changes, and the over exploitation of our earth by us greedy humans. Good luck to us all.

A THREE RELIGION CITY

Many cities of the world have rich religious histories. However none of them can out do the history of Jerusalem. For thousands of years this city has undergone somewhat continual strife. Thousands upon thousands of humans have met their demise due to the cause of religion in this most holy place. Located in the Middle East about 760 meters above sea level it is surrounded by valleys and dry riverbeds. It possesses a very nice cool running spring (Gihon Spring) and was a great place for defense purposes. Nobody knows exactly when it was first settled but ceramic pieces have been dated there to 4,000 B.C.E. It is possible that it was founded as a city by the West Semitic people as early as 2,600 B.C.E. Our little study of the area will start around 1,000 B.C.E when it is possible that David took over the city from the Jebusites. We will finish the adventure with modern day Jerusalem. Today its population is roughly 750,000 and still has 3 main religious groups. It is about 68% Jewish, 30% Muslim, and 2% Christian. However over 3,000 years ago it was occupied by the warlike Jebusites which were named after Jebus which was ancient Jerusalem. They unfortunately were surrounded at this time by 2 rival kingdoms. One was the northern Kingdom of Israel, ruled by Ishbaal. The other was the southern Kingdom of Judah, ruled by David. Yes the Jews were back as previously shown. Before you knew it Ishbaal was murdered and David became also the King of Israel. He wanted to make Jerusalem his capital and that he did. He may have just replaced the Jebusite king and left the inhabitants to stick around for awhile. But what he did do was move the Ark of the Covenant to the city. It probably was a chest that contained tablets of the Jewish laws. It may have been surmounted by 2 golden cherubim with outstretched wings forming the back of a throne for their god Yahwew. It obviously was pretty impressive but it is lost to history. During his reign David started the job of really making Jerusalem the capital of an empire. When he died his son Solomon took over around 970 B.C.E. He had built all kinds of

fabulous buildings with Solomon's Temple being the best of all.
It was to host the Ark of the Covenant and modern excavations
are slowly putting together what it looked like. But the main thing
was that it was built on Mount Zion to give worshippers an
experience of God. All that worked for a good many years but
around 586 B.C.E. the Babylonians popped in and conquered
Jerusalem. To do things right they wiped out Solomon's Temple.
One can blame good old Nebuchadnezzar on that move! The
Jews were exiled to Babylon. They were allowed to return in 538
B.C.E. and they then built the Second Temple, which was
completed in 516 B.C.E. Then along comes Alexander the Great
and in 332 B.C.E. takes over Jerusalem. The Macedonians took
over but all kinds of problems and revolts occurred. However the
Jews stuck around during the revolts etc. In 168 B.C.E. they were
able to make Jerusalem their capital once again. Things flowed
for many years but in 63 B.C.E. General Pompey captures the city
for Rome. The Jews still retain their culture and then along comes
Jesus. More will be devoted to him at a later time. However
suffice it to say things are slowly about to change for our planet.
Anyway Herod the King gets involved and has Jerusalem undergo
a big building transformation. He had built walls, towers, palaces,
and courtyards. The Jewish population and the Romans
maintained somewhat of a balanced equilibrium but by 66 C.E.
the Jews revolted leading to the first Jewish-Roman War. That
probably was not a very bright idea as the Romans brought in
60,000 professional soldiers. By the summer of 70 C.E. the
Roman army had breached the walls of Jerusalem destroying the
city and also the Second Temple. According to the great historian
Josephus about 1,100,000 people were killed along with 97,000
captured. These figures of course are unsubstantiated but we
know thousands of Jews were crucified. The first crucifixions
were actually performed by the Greeks, and Alexander the Great
really liked them. They would just use a vertical beam with the
victim just hanging there until dead. The Romans started using
this procedure for slaves and non-Romans. However they added a
horizontal beam in which the poor guy was roped to his forearms.

They also placed a board on it so the feet could support the body. They would put 1 nail into each foot and slam it into the lower board. The victim would then just stand there and slowly the body would droop. Severe thirst and pain was felt and it usually took 2 – 3 days to die. If he was somewhat lucky they would break his ribs and legs to hasten his ultimate demise. It was not good to be Jewish in any of the areas around Jerusalem. Now by 130 C.E. Hadrian entirely Romanized Jerusalem and named it *Aelia Capitolina*. Jews were banned and this continued until the 300s. Around this time period the Roman Emperor Constantine 1 along with his mother made many new Christian sites most notably the Church of the Holy Sepulchre. He really wasn't a Christian but his mother got into this religion. Slowly more and more Christians came to Jerusalem and Roman rule faded from the scene. With the help of the Jews, Persians (today's Iranians) fought the city and in 614 C.E. took it over. To be nice the Jews were allowed to slaughter the Christians. But by 638 C.E. the Arabs had taken the city and they actually protected any remaining Christians. They built by 701 C.E. the al-Agso Mosque and also the Dome of the Rock was built over the Foundation Stone. This area had deep Jewish significance but Muslims believed it was here that Muhammad ascended to Heaven and met up with figures from the Bible. While there he also spoke to Allah and discussed worship. That of course is quite interesting since Muhammad while living never visited Jerusalem and this holy city is never even mentioned in the Qur'an. Anyway so it goes. Over the next 400 years various Arab groups would control the city. In 1010 C.E. the Caliph al-Hakim orders the destruction of the synagogues and churches. Now one may think that this led to the Crusades but such is not true. It was more like the Byzantine Emperor Alexius Comnenus was having problems with the Turks and he told Pope Urban II that the Muslims were barring Christians from holy sites around Jerusalem. So here comes the Crusades and in 1099 C.E. Duke Godfrey de Bouillon led 1,200 knights and 10,000 infantry in a fight with about 20,000 Muslims. Once the battle was over Jerusalem was a city of

Muslim blood. Jews were also murdered by the Europeans during the battles. The city was in Christian hands but things were not exactly good to go forever. In fact all in all there were a total of 12 Crusades that ended in 1444 C.E. During 1187 C.E. the great Muslim Commander Saladin commanding a 20,000 man army got the Christian King Guy of Jerusalem to fight out of the city. He had 1,200 knights and 18,000 infantry. What he did not have was water, and in the intense heat after a long march the Christians were parched. Saladin ruled the day and took over Jerusalem. He even allowed Jews back in 1187 C.E. Richard the Lion Heart tries to take back the city in 1192 C.E. but fails. However a treaty is signed allowing Christians to come back and worship at their religious sites. So for many years things swing back and forth for the city but in 1517 C.E. the Ottoman Turks take over the city and actually hold it into the 1900's. During the 16th and 17th century the walls were rebuilt and the city expanded. During the 1840's English and German Protestants came and actually constructed new homes and buildings inside the old and new areas of the city. Wealthy Muslims built villas and small waves of Jews from Europe and Russia arrived around 1860. More Christians moved in and then along came World War I. The British army took over the city in 1917 and the League of Nations ultimately told the Brits to establish a "Jewish National Home". They were also to help out the Muslim Palestinians in the area. Things moved slowly and along came World War II. After the war the British Mandate expired and Muslims fought and took over the Old City expelling all Jews. From 1948 until 1949 the Jews fought the "War of Liberation". The Jews prevailed but did not take over the Old City. A treaty was signed dividing the city with the Arabs and Israel was founded in 1949. The Jews made Jerusalem their capital. The Arabs decided to attack Israel in 1967 and the Six Day War was fought against forces of Jordan, Syria, and Egypt. The Jews won and after heavy fighting took over the Old City. Such is Jerusalem today in the hands of the Jewish people. However one should stay tuned to the future.

CLONING LINCOLN

Ok so they did it a number of years ago. They took the DNA out of a cell of a 6-year-old adult Finn Dorset sheep. They took the DNA out of an egg cell from a female sheep and slipped the adult's DNA into that egg. They implanted the egg into a receptive female and in less than 5 months later Dolly was born. She was an exact clone of the original adult. The era of mammalian cloning was born in 1996. Finn Dorset sheep tend to live about 12 years but Dolly only survived for 6 years. She had developed arthritis and a fairly common sheep form of lung cancer. Is it possible that upon birth she already had 6-year-old DNA in her, which limited her life span? Well of course her DNA was that old since it was taken from an adult sheep but that still does not necessarily relate to her demise. She was seriously overweight from lack of exercise, which could have led to arthritis. Her lung cancer was caused by a retrovirus that tends to affect sheep kept mostly indoors. However, ruling out older DNA is impossible in regards to her shortened life span. Nevertheless we have now cloned cows, horses, and even dogs. It will only be a matter of time before we may clone you, the human. If that is in the picture why not clone Abraham Lincoln? We have specimens of his blood and hair, which contains cells preserving his DNA. They are currently attached to skull fragments and various garments but the DNA could be extracted. New techniques will allow us to make a complete genetic map of his DNA producing 46 chromosomes which may ultimately be implanted into a human egg whose own DNA has been removed. However before this is attempted it will be necessary to perhaps remove a bad gene he may have possessed on chromosome 10. Recent investigations are trying to verify if Lincoln was actually dying from cancer when he was assassinated. Booth of course shot him with a derringer with the bullet entering his left ear and lodging behind his right eye. He died at the age of 56 and had been in failing health. During the war years he became increasingly thin and towards 1865 he had headaches, sweats, nausea, and fainting episodes. Unfortunately the autopsy conducted was only of his head and not his bodily organs. It is quite possible that he had inherited a condition known as multiple endocrine neoplasia type 2B (MEN 2B). In this genetic condition almost everyone ultimately develops cancer either in the thyroid or the adrenal glands. It is extremely rare but those with MEN 2B typically show various physical conditions. They tend to be tall in stature. Abe was 6 foot 3.75 inches tall, which was rare in those days. They also have droopy eyelids, bumpy upper lips, an asymmetrical skull shape, and low muscle tone. He possessed all of these characteristics. The intestines contain bumpy growths and Abe was constipated most of his life. MEN 2B is a dominant genetic trait that means if one of his parents had the single gene mutation then there would be a 50% chance of all of the offspring getting the bad gene. Abe's mother died at the age of 34 supposedly from drinking poisonous milk. It was thought that the family cow had eaten the white snakeroot plant (*Ageratina altissima*). This plant contains a very strong poison smelling like turpentine called tremetol. Upon consumption it can get into the cow's milk. Many people were poisoned from it in Illinois in the 1800's. Abe's mother had the features of her son and actually may have died from MEN 2B, which however would be impossible to prove. However it is known that his father did not have MEN 2B features so it is possible she may have suffered from this condition. Most people having MEN 2B die young but not always. To go into a further investigative study Abe had 4 sons. Eddie had Abe's features and died at the age of 3 years 11 months. His death was due to what at that time they called chronic consumption whatever that means. Willie died at the age of 11 probably from scarlet fever. However he also had MEN 2B type lips. Tad died at the age of 18 due to progressive respiratory distress. He also had MEN 2B lips and it is possible he had thyroid cancer that may have caused fluid build up in the heart and lungs. His oldest son Robert lived to 82 and had none of the features attributed to Lincoln. The only way to prove if Abe had MEN 2B is if science has access to his DNA, which will probably ultimately happen. Now to continue the cloning issue one should certainly be aware that it will continue in animals. We are cloning bull cows that are superior in size and in beef marbling. Stud thoroughbred horses are being cloned. A couple in the United States is offering 150,000 dollars for the cloning of their failing 15-year-old dog. However currently most research is investigating the potential of using embryonic stem cells to help cure the human condition. Stem cells are cells, which have not undergone any differentiation. In other words they have not been stimulated to become nerve cells, pancreatic cells, etc. The best stem cells are obtained from the inner cell mass of a blastocyst. This is a 4 – 5 day early stage embryo consisting of 50 – 150 cells. They can be stored in liquid nitrogen that stops all cellular activity for years. Research all over the world is learning how to activate these cells into becoming any of the 200 or so cell types found in humans. Currently in the United States, Federal laws prohibit the usage of Federal funds for working with new embryonic cells lines. This is not true of many other nations and individual companies are allowed to fund studies. Many individuals believe this Federal law is flawed since hundreds of embryos are destroyed every year through incineration. Typically if a couple plans on producing embryos for in vitro fertilization they undergo a procedure producing many embryos. Perhaps 4 or so may be implanted into the uterus with the hope that at least 1 will develop into a baby. The rest are stored in liquid nitrogen perhaps for a future pregnancy. No laws exist for their storage or disposal and usually a charge occurs for storage. Many are simply stored for a period of time and then incinerated usually but not always with the couple's permission. Many scientists believe that those, which will be incinerated, should be utilized for making embryonic cell lines. Finally in 2009 the FDA has approved for the first time testing humans with embryonic stem cells that have been made into oligodendrocytes. Thousands of humans suffer from spinal cord paralysis and this study will take 8 – 10 individuals and inject into the site of injury these stem cells. They will receive the injections for 7 – 14 days with the hope these cells will attach and grow repairing the damaged myelinated sheath surrounding the damaged nerves. As has happened in test animals this procedure allows the damaged nerves to repair themselves restoring nerve signaling and rejuvenation. Unfortunately since these cells came from another human they will have to take anti-rejection medicine but perhaps not for life. Of course it is well known that each individual has attached to their own cells protein "self" markers attached to their cell membranes so that our own cells are not destroyed by our own immune system. The "self" markers on these stem cells are different and so anti-rejection medicine must be taken which unfortunately slows down their immune system in the long run. But hope may be soon around the corner since we are trying to grow pigs whose cells and organs lack the "self" protein markers. In other words since pig parts are of human size and work the same we may someday receive a heart, liver, etc from a porker which may make us well but oink a lot. The future is approaching rapidly and big changes in helping humans are only a matter of time.

WHY ARE WE SOMETIMES EVIL

It has been estimated that roughly one-half of male rhesus monkeys in the wild survive to adulthood. Of course accidents do happen but typically this is due to violent encounters with other males. Young male groups of the common chimpanzee will readily kill another male chimpanzee that is from another group. So is violence in primates wired into our genetic patterns? Why in the world do humans fight wars and kill each other so easily? Well Harvard author and anthropologist Richard Wrangham writes that modern humans are, "the dazed survivors of a continuous, 5 million-year habit of lethal aggression". Evolutionary biologist Dale Peterson, argues, "that on the most basic level, primate (and therefore human) violence is driven by the need to survive and procreate. The best fighters, the ones who wield violence most successfully, are the most likely to survive". Both feel that homicide committed by roving bands of young males can be seen as somewhat of a primitive form of war. It may be committed by one group as a way of weakening a rival community. On a vast scale full-scale wars may be undertaken to take over an entire rival population. Survival of the fittest as Darwin once explained so well. This most certainly is true but violent acts may be possibly attributed somewhat to how early hominins controlled the "cheaters" of their group. Cooperation in the group was extremely important in maintaining a solid cohesiveness. The cheater was one who took without giving. To the extreme was the psychopath who is incapable of empathizing with others. They lack the ability of feeling guilty or remorseful of what they have done. But it is generally just the cheater or noncooperators that had to be controlled by the group. Many evolutionary biologists believe that extreme violence did not begin until humans had the ability to throw long-distance spears. This may sound weird but the spear allowed one to harm another without the risk of hand-to-hand combat. The group could more easily take care of the cheater or the psychopath with less risk of harm. Actually the fossil record shows little evidence of substantial intergroup warfare before 40,000 years ago. We sure have digressed a lot if that is indeed true. It is estimated that about 9% of people were killed by their own social group in the 13th century. This figure dropped to about 4% in the 19th century. But to put that in perspective one must look into the 20th century where at least 42 million people were killed in wars. But unfortunately 170 – 360 million were killed by their own governments. We sure can be a violent bunch but for the average modern human committing a violent act is far from being a normal occurrence. So why are some people evil or violent in nature. Is it deeply seated in their genes or is it an environmental issue? The answer to this is complex and most certainly involves genes and upbringing. Ones upbringing is somewhat of a given so perhaps it is best to look at our genes. Well over 80% of all homicides are committed by men. Most of the victims are also men. Men it is well known secrete ample amounts of the hormone testosterone throughout their lives. Women secrete it in very small amounts, as estrogen is their hormonal thing. Men do produce small amounts of this female hormone. The production of testosterone in men is somewhat certainly governed by a number of genes. However, many testosterone gene receptors exist in our cells and so overall concentrations of circulating testosterone does not necessarily show how much is being utilized by the body. Of course it is well known that in most animals their testosterone levels go up during the mating season. This in many cases leads to high aggressiveness for the dominance of mating. In humans this does not apply as easily. Actually in humans it has been difficult to show a high relationship between high testosterone levels and aggressiveness. It is true though that many males who seek dominating behavior or even high-risk behavior tend to have high circulating testosterone levels. Actually the hormone serotonin may be a better subject to examine in aggressiveness. Once again this hormone is a major signaling agent for our brain cells. Studies have shown that many men with low circulating levels of serotonin are more aggressive in nature than those with higher circulating levels. Other studies have linked men with a history of impulsively violent behavior such as arsonists and violent criminals with low levels of this important hormone. Perhaps we should put all of these characters on prozac! Now how serotonin may somewhat regulate nasty behavior is extremely complex and is only now being somewhat examined. It is a tough study since serotonin in the brain controls activities such as appetite, sleep, memory, and even learning. It also is involved with mood, sexual and hallucinogenic behavior. Remember we have over 100 billion brain cells and each serotonin secreting neuron exerts an influence over as many as 500,000 neurons. The entire development of each individual's brain as we grow and mature is a complex genetic and environmental nightmare for psychiatrists. Only time will tell when the problems of aggressiveness and violence will be readily understood. But to be sure we certainly can be a crazy person. Take for example the recent stabbing and beheading in Canada by an individual who had recently immigrated to Canada from China. Vince Weiguang Li was not known to have anger or emotional problems according to a pastor who hired him while in Canada.

But on a Wednesday night on a bus he suddenly pulled out a knife and stabbed a 22-year old carnival worker named Tim McLean many times to death as passengers looked on. Poor Tim was sitting next to Vince and was in the wrong place at the wrong time. Not to be finished Vince then quickly severed Tim's head and displayed it to the horrified passengers who were fleeing the bus. He then started to hack off pieces of the body and began eating them. When he was finally subdued police officers found a plastic bag in his pocket containing Tim's ear, nose, and part of his mouth. The only thing Vince had to say to the officers was: "I have to stay on the bus forever". Now most psychiatrists would call that "affective" meaning highly emotional aggression. Another type of aggression has been titled "non-affective" or cold-blooded attack. Such was probably the case for the well-known killers who terrorized the area around Washington D.C. in 2002. The killers were John A. Williams and 15-year-old Lee Boyd. John changed his name to John Muhammad when he converted to Islam and was a member of the Nation of Islam. He sort of adopted Lee in Jamaica and was obviously a major influence on him. Lee was a smart kid who took AP courses in high school for a short time. During the overall period 15 individuals were murdered and 7 wounded. They were mostly shot in the back or the head by a Bushmaster XM15E25 .223 rifle. Most of the shots were fired through a hole in the back of the trunk of a 1990 blue Chevrolet Caprice. The first victim around Washington D.C. was James D. Martin who was a churchgoer, PTA member, and a mentor to inner-city kids. He was shot in the back while walking to a supermarket. The bullet severed his spinal cord and opened up his aorta. Then James L. "Sonny" Buchanan was killed while cutting lawn at an auto dealer. Three more individuals were killed that day. One was pumping gas and another was sitting on a bench. The 3rd victim was vacuuming a minivan. Within 18 more days 4 more were killed and 3 wounded. The nation was shocked and the killings would probably have continued but their jig was up. Muhammad had much earlier tested his rifle in the state of Washington at the home of Robert Holmes. Muhammad had also said to Holmes that Lee Malvo was his "little sniper". Holmes watched all the horrific deaths and felt that Muhammad was involved in the murders. This was partly due to the fact that Muhammad's ex-wife lived near D.C. and Muhammad wanted to kill her. Finally he was given an audience with the FBI to tell his story. More things came together as a fingerprint of Malvos was found on a gun catalog left at any earlier murder. Soon the Chevrolet Caprice was found to have been recently purchased by Muhammad. The word hit the air waves to be on the lookout for that car and luckily within hours a Pennsylvania individual spotted it at night in a rest area on I-70 beyond Frederick, Maryland on the east slope of South Mountain. Ultimately a diverse team of authorities and a swat team charged into the car and caught the sleeping murderers without incident. Why would they commit these horrible acts? Perhaps it was because they wanted our government to give them the 10 million dollars they had asked for recently. Perhaps it was a cover so that Muhammad could sneak up and kill his ex-wife. Well young Lee Malvo said he just wanted to "shock and horrify the community" and that he hated white people. Some of the victims were of other ethnicities it should be noted. Malvo also said he liked Muhammad since he found him for "a search for knowledge". Muhammad has remained silent on the subject. Perhaps they were just a couple of non-affective individuals.

LIVING FOREVER

Well that probably just will never happen at least for the foreseeable future. Free radicals are always about doing their damage to our cells. Our mitochondrial DNA slowly but assuredly gets highly damaged leading to less energy production. Every time our cells divide the tips of our chromosomes get snipped a bit and slowly get smaller as we age. Long-lived cells suffer slow yet continuous damage. Actually in recorded history the oldest lived human was Jeanne Louise Calment who died August 4, 1997. She was 122 years old. She once stated, "in life one sometimes makes bad deals". Actually in many ways it might be a good idea to have a very slow metabolism in regards to some longevity. The oldest documented living plant was a great basin bristlecone pine tree *(Pinus longaeva)*. It lived in eastern Nevada for about 5,000 years until a graduate student doing research and U.S. Forest Service personnel cut it down in 1964. They sort of did not know it was the granddaddy of trees! Actually some plant lovers may say that actually there exists a quaking aspen groove in Utah that is 80,000 years old. But this is actually a sprouting (clonal) organism in which aspen trees sprout from a huge root system and the individual trees and their roots actually are short lived as far as trees goes. From the standpoint of the animal kingdom we tend to think that tortoises and Maine lobsters can live a long life. However they are nowhere near the long life experience of the quahog clam *(Arctica islandia)*. I am sure it does not realize it but recently one was dug up from the seabed off of Iceland and sclerochronologists estimate its age at around 400 years. These folks can figure this out by studying their growth rings, which is what they do for a life. 400 years is a very long life for animal cells even living in cold conditions and scientists are studying these critters trying to find their key to long survival. Conclusions from this study may help but humans sure have figured out ways to shorten our life span and the life span of countless other species. The Japanese may be considered to be of interest in how we sometimes play with our demise. Probably the brightest group of humans it is a wonder why a select few of them test fate by having a dinner of fugu. Fugus are pufferfish and the most prized one on the market is the tiger pufferfish *(Takifugu rubripes)*. Fugu is a delicacy in parts of the orient and it only comes with one problem. It can be extremely poisonous containing various degrees of a poison known as tetrodotoxin (TTX). All it does is paralyze your body but since it cannot penetrate one's brain you remain awake but paralyzed. It may lead to death and about 50 Japanese die each year from eating a tasty dinner. Pufferfish along with various other marine organisms acquire this poison from their aquatic food chain with certain marine bacteria being the first in the chain to produce it. It accumulates in their skin, liver, intestine, and even the ovaries.

TTX serves as a selective advantage to those that contain it since other animals tend to avoid eating those, which contain TTX. Of course all species that contain it have evolved an evolutionary gene adaptation so that they themselves are not poisoned by their own poison. Oh by the way TTX is not found in the muscle meat of the pufferfish so if the poisonous parts are removed then the fish is a tasty morsel. They must be since the Japanese have been consuming pufferfish for over 2,300 years! I am sure there was a lot of early experimentation and disasters before deaths slowed down. It is actually a pretty nasty way to get poisoned. Upon consumption of the poisonous parts one experiences dizziness, nausea, headache, malaise, paralysis, and possibly death from respiratory failure. Still thousands like to take the chance but fortunately since 1958 only specially licensed chefs can prepare it. They have to take a 2 – 3 year study and still only 30% become licensed chefs. Unfortunately many home amateurs like to carefully remove the poisonous parts often with deleterious results. So it goes. We humans currently are also trying our best to negate the life spans of a tremendous amount of the earth's plant and animal populations. One could easily devote a 10,000-page book on that subject alone. Suffice it to say a few examples might be of order. The blue finned tuna (*Thunnus thynnus)* is the largest of the 40 or so tuna species. It may reach 10 feet long in size and weigh around 1,500 pounds. The largest one caught with fishing tackle weighed 1,496 pounds and was caught off of Nova Scotia in 1979. They may live up to 50 years, swim over 30 mph, and travel thousands of miles during their migrations. We used to catch so many of them that many of the juveniles were used for cat food. Currently over fishing has decimated them by 97% of their 1960 population. By the way killer whales and pilot whales also prey upon them. They are indeed at risk of extinction but we are still-hunting them for whatever the cost. A recent 282-pound specimen just sold in Japan for 100,000 dollars just to be made into expensive sushi. Only a hard to believe conservation effort is likely to save them. Humans also tried their best to wipe out the largest animal to ever live on the earth. The blue whale

(*Balaenoptera musculus*) is larger than even the largest dinosaur. It may reach over 110 feet long and weigh more than 200 tons. Their heart can weigh a hefty 1,320 pounds! They might eat up to 40 million krill a day and survive for 80 years. During the whaling years we killed 378,200 or so of these critters. It was estimated that before whaling began about 239,000 blue whales existed in the Antarctic alone. Currently only a little over 2,400 exist. The total population of all subspecies is probably around 5,000 – 12,000 but the Antarctic ones are the largest of the group. Regarding the Antarctic population humans may once again possibly lead to their extermination. This may also apply to the Arctic population, which numbers less than 1,000 individuals. During the winter the polar ice sheets trap huge amounts of algae that are a major food source of krill. Krill are actually small crustaceans related to shrimp and are in high abundance in these frigid waters. In their oceanic niche krill depend on the summer time melt to free vast supplies of algae for their growing seasons. This heavy feeding time produces tremendous amounts of krill. Unfortunately global warming is causing the global ice sheets to melt at unprecedented rates. This is likely to change the ecosystem patterns in these areas disrupting the normal feed cycles thereby lowering krill populations. Of possible further insult one may want to look back to an interesting movie from 1973. Known as Soylent Green it was based on an overpopulated world where normal food was scarce and people tended to eat wafers made from soybeans and lentils (Soylent red and yellow). The big kicker in the movie was the company making this product came out with a green wafer called Soylent Green. By the film's ending this wafer was found to be made from processed dead people! Now going back to current times there is much talk of harvesting our substantial krill populations to be made into nutritious foodstuffs perhaps resembling wafers. This is for human consumption and makes sense due to their high nutritional value. High in protein, minerals and omega – 3 fatty acids krill would make an excellent food source. It does not look real good for the future of the blue whale. Containing over 98% of the same

DNA as humans the mountain gorilla *(Gorilla beringei beringei)* is also in deep trouble on planet earth. Only about 700 are known to exist. We have never been able to get them to reproduce in captivity and none are currently found in any zoos. One reason for their lack of mating is that they are particularly particular in whom they wish to mate with. If a male does not like the female they just will not mate and visa versa. Now mountain gorillas can get pretty big with the males sometimes reaching 6 feet tall and weigh up to 500 pounds. They eat so much plant material that according to a 1949 study they get 5,000 mgs of vitamin C per day. They are currently found in isolated groups in Central Africa and the Congo. If left alone their lifespan could possibly be up to 50 years but things are shaky at best for their survival. Habitat loss and disease is a threat along with poaching. Some have been killed so that their heads and hands can be sold illegally. Their hands have been made into cigarette ashtrays. Perhaps their major current threat is war and civil unrest especially in the Democratic Republic of Congo. In the Congo Tutsi rebels and government militias have been fiercely fighting displacing over 200,000 refuges. 200 of the world's remaining mountain gorillas live in the rebels hiding grounds and nobody is able to protect these primates. Elephants, hippos, buffalos, and antelope are being killed for food and nobody knows the ultimate fate of the gorillas. Only time will tell their future and unfortunately the future of countless other species as the world continues its quest for craziness.

THE FAITH

It can sure be tough on an individual if he or she survives long enough in life to be able to think about existence. The fortunate ones who stay healthy into their elderly years still recognize the fact that soon their time will be up on earth. Then what happens one may ponder? Do we just go back to being a huge assortment of elements and compounds going back into such things as the nitrogen and phosphorous cycles? It is perhaps better politics and hope for the best by believing in some sort of after-life. This would make sense since if existence exists, which it does, then why not a continuation of it once we get old and tired. It really makes sense if we are young and fall off a mountain or get blasted by a bullet in some sort of strange war. We naturally tend to hope for the best and so all we have left is some kind of faith. The problem with faith is that we just do not know what the ultimate outlook is all about. But for many it gives us a sort of peace of mind knowing that our beliefs may be true and that by following them good things will happen on earth and further up the alley. True faith certainly leads many to lead a better life in regards to how we deal with our trials and tribulations. It may make us make better decisions as to how to deal with our fellow mankind and just how to be nice while on our individual journey. So as how has been earlier shown various faiths have popped up and for many we can only hope for the best. Obviously where you were born and raised has a dramatic influence on where ones faith may start. If one perhaps was born in a part of India you might have gotten into Jainism as your religion. About 4.2 million Jains are hanging out on the earth as we speak. They believe that all living organisms possess a soul and that the universe was never created, nor will it ever cease to exist. A fly is considered to be sacred as well as garlic, onions, and potatoes along with all other organisms. Being vegetarians many Jains will not eat foods such as garlic, onions, and potatoes. The reason is quite simple. In order to eat them the entire plant is killed and that is a no no. Now here is an example of another interesting religion. If one was born somewhat recently in a country like Jamaica perhaps you became a Rastafarian. Founded in the 1920's and 30's Rastafari believe in the divinity of the once Ethiopian Emperor Haile Selassie I. It is quite historically possible that Ethiopa thousands of years ago became a haven for certain Old Testament people. Selassie upon becoming Emperor took the titles of "Lion of the Tribe of Judah, Elect of God, and King of the Kings of Ethiopia. To the founder of this movement this was a clear fulfillment of Revelation 5:5 and Ezekiel 28:25. Rastifarians had found the true "Messiah". Typical Rastafarian lifestyle includes ritual use of marijuana, avoidance of alcohol, the wearing of a dreadlock hairstyle, and vegetarianism. Bob Marley (1945 – 1981) is well known to many as the most famous Rastifarian bringing reggae music to a worldwide audience. Shortly before his death due to cancer this amazing musician was baptized into the Ethiopian Orthodox Church. So it goes. Now religious beliefs encompass an entire global scenario and perhaps you were born on the South Pacific island of Tanna. You might just be into the religion of Jon Frum. The locals were into a god named Kerapenmun who was associated with the extinct volcano Tukosmeru. But around the days of early World War II cargo planes came to the South Pacific and the locals were in awe of this new spectacle. Various leaders took it upon themselves to promise that American World War II servicemen (Jon Frum types) will arrive with their cargo planes with promises of houses, food, clothes, and transport. A native named Manehivi promised the dawn of a new age in which missionaries would leave their islands. This bunch of individuals believes that John Frum is "our God, our Jesus" and that he will come on a February 15th. By the way he has not shown up yet but the South Pacific is currently being invaded by swarms of Mormons trying with some success to make this the religion of the region. One certainly could make it a lifetime adventure studying the religions past and present of our world. However, the big one of course in current times is Christianity although Islam is getting bigger and bigger. Many in the world look at Christianity as "The Faith". There is no doubt that Jesus existed and lived around Jerusalem. It has been well documented that during his years the people living in the area expected a great figure from the past to return. The Old Testament as such did not exist as a book but there were plenty of laws, stories, and poetry readings available to be studied and discussed. Actually prophesies of a coming Messiah had been thought about for over 1,000 years. People in this area certainly thought that "God" had promised King David that he would "establish the throne of his kingdom forever" (2 Sam. 7:13). Of course the major population in this area was Jewish in nature with most of the people being somewhat commoners as such. One specific party group though was the

Pharisees who had been around since about 135 B.C.E. Many were religious teachers and experts who believed in repentance and forgiveness and were actually quite popular. About 4,000 individuals were Essenes who were the lay people and priests who wrote the Dead Sea Scrolls. Sadducees also existed who literally followed old Jewish texts and were actually sort of a political party. They were closely associated with the Temple until it was destroyed in 70 C.E. Although the Jewish population was generally given lots of freedom they were under the control of the Romans. In fact at the time of Jesus the Roman frontiers ran for over 10,000 miles with control of over 80,000,000 human individuals. But as is well known Jesus more than any other individual in world history slowly but surely changed the nature of much of human history. This is quite amazing for a man in which not all that much is known. But from his life and deeds came the New Testament from which countless humans literally interpret as the word of God. However from a historical perspective one perhaps should look at the evolution of this book. It has been argued as to where he was born and on what date. The 4 Gospels differ in the account of his birth with neither Mark nor John even mentioning the event. Matthew and Luke say he was born in Bethlehem when King Herold the Great was alive. Luke further states that the event occurred around the time that Caesar Augustus sent out a decree that the entire known world should be taxed. This taxing was first made when Quirinius was governor of Syria. What causes problems with Luke's writings is that the famous historian Josephus in his massive history dated between 75 and 80 C.E. showed that Quirinius was the governor of Syria in 6 C.E. when the Judean providence was brought under Roman rule. It is known that King Herold the Great died either in 4 or 5 B.C.E. Rome had not taken over the area around Jerusalem by this time and so there was no taxation by Rome itself during his reign. It is even possible that later the taxation of the Jews in this area never really occurred. It is true though that Caesar Augustus levied a tax on Roman citizens around this time to help pay for his armies. But we do know from Josephus that a local census was taken in 6 C.E. It is quite possible that this census was for taxation to the Jewish people now under Roman rule. However Roman taxation policies were that all citizens should be taxed in their own cities. It is well known that Jesus was the son of Mary and Joseph who actually lived in the area of Nazareth in Galilee, which was not under direct Roman rule. Luke places the birth of Jesus in Bethlehem since Joseph and Mary were required to go there for the census. The most likely reason for Bethlehem is that this "the city of David" would be the proper birthplace for a future Messiah. It is highly doubtful from a legal standpoint that Mary and Joseph would have had to make this journey. Now Matthew's Gospel birth is a bit different with it occurring in Bethlehem under King Herold's reign. This gospel professes that after the birth they then traveled and lived in Nazareth. They moved there since it was unsafe in other areas due to the reign of terror by King Herold in the murdering of Jewish sons. It is quite difficult to also validate this path of the birth of Jesus. However Matthew does throw into the idea of a bright star directly over Bethlehem at the time of the birth. This may actually show a scientific timetable for the birth of Jesus. We know from astronomer evidence of this time period that a large bright comet was observed in Rome and in many areas of the world in 12 B.C.E. We also now know that this was the famous Halley's comet. This was actually the same year that Herold's Temple was finished and that he was still alive. We also know that many dignitaries from all over came during that year to celebrate the finishing of the temple. Could it possibly be considered that the 3 wise men of the New Testament were actually dignitaries bringing gifts to Jerusalem? Nobody of course knows but this is a quite interesting question. If indeed the comet plays a role in the time of the birth then Jesus was born probably in Nazareth in 12 B.C.E. Josephus places the arrest of John the Baptist between 33 and 34 C.E. He of course was arrested and later beheaded by Antipas the ruler of Galilee. He did not like the fact that John criticized him for marrying his sister-in-law Herodias. Jesus started his ministry shortly after the beheading and according to the book of John he ministered through 3

Passovers. Of course he was crucified during the 3rd one. Since Passover is fixed by the new moon he was then crucified on March 30, 36 C.E. He would have been 48 years old. Now this date is not a sure fact as others believe he died on Friday April 7, 30 C.E. Of interest it was very rare unless you were a celibate Essene not to be a married Jew. Could it have actually have been possible that Mary Magdalene was actually Jesus' wife and that he possibly had children? Unfortunately we probably will never know the answer to that question. However, we do know that indeed he was crucified and what is strange is that he died in about 3 hours. This is an extremely quick death for those on a cross. His death was observed by Mary Magdalene and his body was claimed by the wealthy Joseph of Arimathea. He placed Jesus' body in a garden tomb and "rolled a great stone to the door of the tomb, and departed (Matt 27:60). Three days later Mary Magdalene and Mary the mother of James went to the tomb and found the stone rolled away and an empty tomb. Here of course is where things get interesting. Did Jesus go to heaven to be with "the Father" or did some individuals just remove his body? For "The Faith" to continue the obvious answer is the heaven thing. Two thousand years later millions upon millions of humans still believe in the Resurrection. Now one asks how the teachings of Jesus and the idea of the Resurrection came to be known to his ultimate followers. From a historical standpoint this is a very difficult question to answer. We know that Jesus did most of his preaching around the Sea of Galilee. During this time period many believe this was a turbulent area known for its extremists and their apocalyptic visions. Perhaps many of his followers wrote down some of his thoughts. His disciples most likely were involved with some writings and they probably told their tales to other writers. Through the early years many writers wrote short passages of parts of his life that were constantly rearranged and interpreted differently. Slowly over time these passages were kind of put together forming "proto-gospels". Actually many different Gospels were actually written. The New Testament of course sticks with Matthew, Mark, Luke, and John. Many religious scholars doubt that these specific individuals actually where the true authors. However, some believe John was real. Nobody knows the exact dates of their writing but most scholars attest to between 60 C.E. to 150 C. E. What is known is that by 180 C.E. they were considered authoritative. Of interest is that they were written in Greek, which may have changed some early interpretations. The Gospels certainly offer differing thoughts on the life of Jesus. However, it is the writings of Paul that produce the foundation of the Church. It appears that Paul found various Disciples of Jesus perhaps only 1 year after his death. He journeyed for many years far and wide spreading "The Faith" and founding churches. He wrote various letters in the New Testament and had others written for him. He focused that Jesus is the living Christ in the form of God. No other individual did more in establishing this religion. So what we see are some thoughts on early Christianity. To be sure Jesus was a wonderful human preaching love, harmony, and how to live a moral life. He has had a profound effect through the ages in helping people lead a life of true harmony with the universe. Unfortunately in many cases the extremists of "The Faith" kind of got things all wrong. The book of Exodus states "thou shall not suffer a witch to live". Paul stated: " men, leaving the natural use of the women, burned in their lust one toward another. They which practice such things are worthy of death". Too bad some people tend to take some things literally. People in much of the Middle Ages harbored fears, superstitions, and just plain strange ideas. In Europe during the 1400s and afterwards the Church was very powerful. During these days any association with the Devil was a big no no. All kinds of things could trigger the witch-hunts that were allowed by both the Catholic and Protestant churches. Crop failures, pestilence, or the death of livestock could be blamed on one's neighbor. In 1424 an unfortunate man was charged with turning himself into a mouse in Rome! Everyone could be suddenly charged as a witch. This was especially true of widows and unmarried females. Even Catholic priests and wealthy merchants ran into big time trouble. All in all perhaps many more than

1,000000 humans were drowned, hanged, or burned in the insanity. Even Martin Luther thought witches were part of the forces of darkness and should be burned as heretics. The protestant reformer John Calvin stated: "The Bible teaches us that there are witches and they must be slain". The founder of the Methodist Church, John Wesley believed anyone who denied the reality of witchcraft was in direct opposition to the Bible. Pope Innocent VIII provided his blessing and encouragement to witch-hunts. In his Bull *Summis desiderantes* written in 1484 he stated: "may exercise against all persons, of whatsoever condition and rank, the said office of inquisition, correcting, imprisoning, punishing and chastising, according to their deserts, those persons they find guilty as aforesaid". So things could and did get pretty crazy. Boils or growths could be areas where the Devil may suck on and were called the "witches teat". Scars, moles, or discolorations could be called the "mark of the beast". In Scotland they thought such marks might be invisible so unfortunates were pricked with needles to see if their skin has an area of insensitivity. People often began their examinations with various means of torture. The unfortunate may have been hung by their wrists using a pulley fixed to the ceiling. Heavy weights were attached to the feet. The body was raised then lowered with a jerk dislocating the arms and legs. One may have been tied to a rack while water was poured down the throat mimicking drowning. Does this sound familiar during modern times? Perhaps cords were tied around the person and tightened eating into the flesh. Sharp irons were used to mangle breasts. Red-hot pincers tore off flesh. Red-hot irons were inserted into the vagina and rectum. Fingernails were ripped off and then needles were sent into the tender fingers. Thumbscrews crushed fingers and toes. Hands were immersed into boiling oil. On the way to the stake or gallows victims were flogged, burned, branded, and often had their hands and tongues hacked off. Humans sure can be scary animals! One of the best was Johann von Dorheim. In the 1600s in Germany this Prince-Bishop of Bamberg had built a special witch-house. It had no windows but cells containing thumbscrews, leg vices, scalding lime baths, and prayer stools containing sharp pegs. He tortured at least 600 humans and then burned them at the stake. The burnings continued well into the 17th century. Fortunately things slowly started to settle down. Greater heads prevailed and the specific churches saw that perhaps they were wrong about the whole thing. They actually got an understanding that it was the extreme tortures that actually got the people to confess their heresies! In fact in 1657 the Roman Catholic Church stated without apology that not a single case of the witch-trial hunts had been conducted properly. So all in all the witch-hunts were a wonderful example of what one might call "blind faith". Too bad many modern religions and humans still harbor many strange thoughts on religion. A final quote from Adolf Hitler in his book Mein Kampf (1927) says it all. "Hence today I believe that I am acting in accordance with the will of the almighty creator: by defending myself against the jews, I am fighting for the work of the Lord".

SOMEONE HAD TO SAVE THE FREE WORLD

He was born at Blenheim Palace in 1874 and was named Winston Leonard Spencer Churchill. The palace was the home of the seventh Duke of Malborough, John Churchill. He was the commander of the armies that defeated the French in various battles at the beginning of the 18th century. John was a rich man and Winston's grandfather. Winston's parents were Lord and Lady Randolph Churchill. Lord Churchill was a Member of Parliament and a politician. His mother was actually American born to a wealthy businessman. He became Prime Minister of Britain in 1940 at the age of 65 and was the leader of these islands during World War II. He quite possibly saved the world from the tyranny of Adolf Hitler's Germany. He was a brilliant man, Victorian in his ways, and believed in the goodness of the world. Evil was evil and was to be dealt with severely. Probably millions of pages have been devoted to Sir Winston Churchill so again this is not the point of dealing with his existence. However he was a warrior in nature and this probably developed at a somewhat early age. He graduated from the Royal Military Academy and was in various cavalry regiments. He was part of many battles with his best being in Africa in 1898. The British had hold of Egypt and was involved in a large battle against 60,000 Arab Deruishes. The 21st Lancers were told to charge into a large group of these ethnic people and he led 25 troopers into battle. They charged into the Dervish forces using mostly lances and swords. Fortunately for Churchill he had previously hurt his shoulder and had to use his mouser pistol for the work ahead. Surrounded by Dervishes he killed at least three and one suddenly came directly at him "with uplifted sword" and the pistol did the job. Finding himself isolated he headed back to his group under fire. A Dervish suddenly sprung out from a concealed hole and charged at him. The pistol came in handy once again and he made it back to his forces. Unfortunately the 21st Lancers suffered a 22 % casualty but the battle was won. Winston Churchill loved the thrill of battle and would not forget his experiences. Later throughout the early 1900's he held many different government positions but by the early 1930's he no longer held any offices or positions. But he was indeed a famous man and was quite outspoken as to the dangers of Germany and Adolf Hitler. He knew the evil in this man and was quite aware of the build up of war- making machinery occurring at all levels in Germany. Britain though refused to build a huge military machine and believed peace with Germany would prevail. Churchill knew better but was in the minority. But the nice thing about living in the 30's for him was that he owned a magnificent countryside estate called Chartwell. Looking over the English Channel it actually has a history going back to the 1300's. He was still able to make money through his writings and had time to think of Hitler. He lived the Victorian life having a cook and 18 servants not to mention various secretaries. Perhaps one might find it interesting as to how he lived a typical day. Typically he lived with his wife and kids and had constant guests and important visitors. He would arise naked somewhere around 8 am and immediately take off his black satin sleep mask. Upon ringing his bell a valet would soon bring him his breakfast starting off with orange juice in a bottle. He did not like squeezed orange juice. A small steak or cutlet would suffice but he always had to have jam with his meal. In fact he would not touch any food until the jam arrived and it was usually black cherry. Then it would be time for a bath and the tub must be two-thirds full with a temperature of 98°F. Upon adjusting to this temperature the valet would have to then make it exactly 104°F! While in the bath he may recite Kipling or rehearse his speeches or lectures. After being dried by the valet he puts on a dressing gown and retires to his bed where he will stay until early afternoon. Conveniently placed beside the bed is a weak 3 oz Johnny Walker Red scotch which he will sip through the morning. Winston Churchill found many years ago a fondness for drink while living in many primitive countries where the water was foul with disease. He will then read 3 papers front to back and have his first of 10 or more giant Cuban cigars. He goes through the morning mail and then perhaps dictates to a secretary letters he wants to send to the government or any other correspondence. He then may receive into his bedchamber various guests. Only the King will not be seen in his bedchamber! He dresses at 1:15 pm and comes down to greet his family. His wife Clementine he calls "cat" and she calls him "pug". His daughter Diana is "puppy kitten" and his son Randolph is "chumbolly". Not to be left out his 2 other daughters Sarah and Mary are respectively called "mule" and "mouse". At lunchtime at a big round table they are seated along with various guests. Lunch is usually Irish stew or Yorkshire pudding and rarely foul. Winston has adopted many of Chartwell's chickens as pets and calls them "his friends". He is great lover of animals. Wine and champagne is usually served with lunch and after eating he has a glass of port with a plain ice. It is then time for him and his friends to talk and out comes the brandy and cigars. He tends to like to talk of serious topics "with myself as chief conversationalist". However anyone can feel free to interject at anytime in the discussions. When the talking was done it then might be time for a stroll around his estate. He loved feeding his golden orfe fish, ducks, swans, and chickens. Ultimately the guests would leave or retire for a while leaving Mr.

Churchill to himself. He would then sit on a favorite wicker chair with a Johnny Walker red and contemplate his world. He may then head to his studio to continue his paintings. A wonderful artist he would finish over 500 works of art. Sometimes he would then roam around the various rooms at Chartwell periodically looking at his collection of pistols and rifles. Then it would be time for a 1 – 2 hour nap. Awaking around 5 pm he would often play cards with his family. At 7 pm he would then take his 2nd bath. While bathing friends might come in for more interesting discussions or he might dictate various thoughts to a secretary. Dining was set for 8:30 pm and what a dinner it would be consisting of several courses. His guests typically might run into clear soup, oysters, caviar, cheeses, pate de fois gras, trout, shoulder of lamb, lobster, dressed crab, pete marmite, scampi, Dover sole, roast beef, chocolate éclairs, and Yorkshire pudding. Of course buckets of iced champagne would be part of the meal. The talk and discussion after dinner would include cigars, port, and brandy. Talk went on until 10 pm or so and the guests would then leave or retire to their rooms for the night. It was then time for Winston Churchill to begin his "working day". In his study with a couple of secretaries he would dictate speeches, magazine articles, or a manuscript for a book. Between 1931 and 1939 he published in volumes more than 400 articles and worked on 368 speeches. His articles and books would typically earn him about $96,000 a year. He often dictated 4,000 – 5,000 words a night and on weekends perhaps over 10,000 words. He would usually work until 3 am or so and then retire for his 5 or so hours of deep sleep. So that was a typical day spent at Chartwell. Of course not all days were such, as he did not spend all his waking moments at his beloved Chartwell. It certainly sounds like a nice existence but then a small matter pressed him back into the service of his country. The invasions of Hitler's Germany in 1939 and 1940 terrified the world and Churchill before you know it became the Prime Minister. He had for years told the free world of Hitler's ambition but most countries just put their head in the sand like an ostrich. Of a side note ostriches do not put their head into the sand when scared. Actually they just lie in the sand and their feather patterns in this position make it look like their head is in the sand! By June 1940 Hitler had control over the vast majority of Western Europe. All that was needed for him to do was to take over the British Isles and victory would be complete. He could then turn his attentions to the hated communists in Eastern Europe. The United States at this time was in no position to militarily help and Britain was in no way prepared militarily to stop Hitler's aggression. Of course they had their powerful navy and wonderful Hurricane and Spitfire fighter planes. But it would take some time to rearm and also get help from the United States. Fortunately a number of factors were in Britain's favor. Germany did not have a sufficient naval fleet to invade the islands. Britain's air force and navy had sufficient power to make an invasion highly difficult. Adolf Hitler also actually wanted a negotiated peace with Britain so that he could go eastward in his destruction. Finally once again Britain had Winston Churchill. Many in the government felt compelled for negotiations with Hitler. They thought they might be able to appease him and avoid a total conflict. Churchill believed heavily in good vs. evil and knew it would only be a matter of time before Britain and her navy would be under German control. His 40-minute oration to the House of Commons says it all. "The battle of France is over. I expect that the battle of Britain is about to begin. Upon this battle depends the survival of Christian civilization. Upon it depends our own British life and the long continuity of our institutions and our Empire. The whole fury and might of the enemy must very soon be turned on us. Hitler knows that he will have to break us in this island or lose the war. If we can stand up to him all Europe may be free, and the life of the world will move forward into broad, sunlit uplands; but if we fail, then the whole world, including the United States, and all that we have known and cared for, will sink into the abyss of a new dark age made more sinister, and perhaps more prolonged, by the lights of a perverted science. Let us therefore brace ourselves to our duty and so bear ourselves that if the British Commonwealth and

Empire lasts for a thousand years, men will still say, 'this was our finest hour'". Of course this famous quotation helped to sway the government to fight to the finish. Churchill also knew that drastic measures needed to be immediately addressed. In order to keep the French fleet from falling into German hands he ordered the sinking of a large portion of the fleet in Northern Africa. Over 1,200 French sailors were killed but this important mission was accomplished. He also knew that he would need the help of the United States that was not ready to join the fight. He stated often to President Roosevelt his urgent need for ships and supplies. He stressed that all will be lost without the total help of the United States. Help would certainly come but it would take some time. Meanwhile during the summer of 1940 Hitler had waves of fighters and bombers attack the airfields of Britain leading to "the Battle of Britain". Both sides lost unsustainable numbers of planes and many airstrips were damaged. But a funny thing happened in the early fall which may be of high importance in the loss of the war for Germany. A German pilot accidentally dropped some bombs on the city of London. To Churchill the bombing of the city even with minimal damage deserved revenge. He ordered bombers to go and bomb Berlin, which was done inflicting little damage to the city. Hitler however lost it and then demanded that instead of attacking airstrips and airplane factories it was the cities that needed destroyed. So the "Blitz" began in earnest and many cities were damaged with lives lost. However this gave Britain time to rebuild their military machinery and increase plane production. Furthermore in 1941 Hitler decided to attack Russia giving Britain even more time to get it together. Ultimately, the United States entered the war and Churchill proclaimed: "No American will think wrong of me if I proclaim that now to have the United States on our side was to me the greatest joy. I could not foretell the course of events. I do not pretend to have measured accurately the martial might of Japan, but now at this very moment I knew the United States was in the war, up to the neck and into the death. So we had won after all"! Of interest is that Churchill spent most of the war in London but still pretty much stuck to his typical daily schedule. However, all his activities were devoted to the war. After dinner typically a movie was watched and then he would retire to his war room until 3 am. He was knighted in 1953 and died at the age of 91 in 1965.

ONCE GOOD NOW REAL BAD

For thousands upon thousands of years humans suffered from all sorts of painful maladies and broken body parts. For those of us living in modern societies we are helpless in trying to figure out how chronically painful was the life of millions of humans. Breaking bones or suffering through chronic illnesses must have just been a horrible experience. However thousands of years ago a somewhat small grouping of the world's population happened upon a plant that helped take the pain away from whatever ailed them. The plant is the poppy *(papaver somniferum)* and it grew wild in Asia Minor. In this area including Turkey, Pakistan, Afganistan, and once Persia the wild poppy blew its tiny seeds all over the place. The plant grew and produced beautiful flowers of which whose petals were not long lasting. Before long the plant would mature and produce a large seedpod containing hundreds of seeds. Somewhere along the line humans must have noticed that if the pod was sliced at a certain time a latex looking liquid would leak out of the pod. Somewhere along the line someone tasted this bitter tasting liquid and soon noticed a slight change occurring inside of them. They felt a little bit better and if they were in pain it was somewhat reduced. Before long they got lots of the liquid and either just drank it or perhaps made it into a tea. Soon they felt much more relaxed, dreamy, and in much less pain. What they discovered was morphine, which of course is highly used today for pain relief in medicine. It not only takes away pain but also to most is a pleasurable experience. The seedpod of this poppy just happens to contain roughly 10 – 15% morphine and 1 – 3% codeine plus some other analgesics. The dried stuff became known as opium. Humans started to cultivate it in Persia, Egypt, and Mesopotamia at least 4,000 years ago. It could be smoked, made into a tea, and also made into all kinds of crazy concoctions. For many early humans it provided the necessary relief from pain and a very hard existence. Its plantings and usage spread with the Romans to much of the known world. It certainly had the positive attributes in early societies to relieve pain, make one feel good, and it even provided relief for all types of common intestinal problems. It was the perfect medicine for early civilizations. Of added benefit its seeds could be ground up and made into a protein rich food. In the 1500's early chemists placed the opium in brandy and made what is called laudanum. Of course they were a bit crazy since some also put frog sperm into this concoction. Alcohol draws out more of the morphine molecules for a stronger substance thereby enhancing its effects. The popularity of opium was incredible. Thomas Sydenham, the father of English medicine wrote: "Among the remedies which it has pleased the Almighty God to give to man to relieve his sufferings, none is so universal and so efficacious as opium." Thomas Jefferson grew it at Monticello and its seeds were sold at the gift shop of Thomas Jefferson for Historic Plants until 1991. It certainly relieved the pain of many soldiers in the Civil War especially during amputations. It did have its problems since thousands became addicted from smoking it for its pleasurable effects. That however did not keep the English pharmacist C.R. Alder Wright from trying to make it into a more powerful pain reliever in 1874. Essentially what he did was boil morphine with acetic acid (concentrated vinegar). Indeed before long he came up with a much more powerful pain reliever and it was names heroin. Heroin ($C_{21}H_{23}NO_5$) was soon marketed by Bayer Pharmaceuticals and became a big hit. Heroin we will soon see can be horribly addicting and before long thousands upon thousands of humans suffered from its addiction. The United States outlawed it in 1905 and even today refuses to use it to ease the pain of dying cancer patients. Most people of course know something about heroin yet still today hundreds of thousands are addicted to it. In 2008 Afghanistan produced so much illegal heroin that they are storing some of it for later illegal sale. Heroin's problem is that it works too well in the human brain. When taken into the body it is made into 6-acetylmorphine, which rapidly enters the brain and attaches to a host of brain receptors. We happen to have a number of opiod receptors because our body makes chemicals very similar to heroin. This morphine substance locks into dopamine receptors causing the body to produce lots of dopamine, which gives us pleasurable feelings. The locking lasts awhile so lots of dopamine floods the brain. The morphine substance also locks into endorphine receptors causing a flood of pain relieving chemicals to flow. These receptors also moderate stress in humans. It also goes to an area of the brain known as the locus coeruleus, which helps to control our sympathetic nervous system by producing norepinephrine. The morphine substance slows the output of norepinephrine giving us feelings of safety and contentment. However this slowing also lowers blood pressure and heart rate. This substance also affects the respiratory center of the brain slowing breathing. Opiod receptors are also in our digestive tract and this substance causes constipation. Finally other brain areas may be affected such as the nucleus accumbens in the forebrain, which deals with reinforcing behaviors. As is well known thousands of people die worldwide from overdosing on heroin. Yet countless people love the drug at first but before long they may become addicted from continual usage. The addiction basically occurs because heroin replaces the natural chemicals that stimulate the production of dopamine, endorphins, etc. Our body basically just quits producing these chemicals and the brain is relying on the morphine substance to stimulate the pathways. If the locus coeruleus does not have the morphine substance it goes into overdrive producing far too much norepinephrine. This leads to anxiety, stress, high blood pressure, and rapid heartbeat. This creates a huge problem for the heroin user. They fear the thought of quitting and worry about the rough withdrawal symptoms if they try to stay off the stuff. Withdrawal symptoms can be very bad and of course there is a biochemical explanation. Withdrawal symptoms typically occur about 12 hours after last usage. They peak in about 2 – 4 days and usually last for around 14 days. However, as will be shown people not taking maintenance medicine may feel bad for about 31 weeks.

Now dealing with the biochemistry a lack of the morphine substance entering the locus coeruleus causes this area to as already been stated go into overdrive. It produces far too much norepinephrine, which again causes, anxiety, stress, high blood pressure, increased respiration, and rapid heartbeat. One may also have sweating, hot/cold flashes, and general restlessness. Ones body temperature also tends to drop. Since one now is hardly producing any dopamine general bad feelings soon develop. The lack of endorphin production may cause pain in areas of the body. It is no wonder one seeks to avoid the pains of withdrawal. Detoxification can certainly help a heroin addict but the average addict actually goes through detox an average of 10 – 15 times during their lives. The initial detox program needs are to seek the patient relief from the symptoms listed above but also including tremors, cramping, chills, nausea, vomiting, and even diarrhea. A number of methodologies are used of which 2 will be examined. One method essentially uses clonidine, buprenorphine, and perhaps an anti-anxiety medicine like clonazepan. The other method, which costs between 7,500 – 15,000 dollars, is ultra-rapid detox under general anaesthesia. This procedure is not without controversy but involves the patient being asleep for 4 hours or more. The patient is given a concoction of medicines including clonidine, naltrexone, and clonazepam. This method allows the patient to receive higher doses of medicines than can usually be tolerated. Clonidine is a blood pressure medicine that slows heart beat and lowers blood pressure. It is used since it works its way to the locus coeruleus region of the brain that is now overproducing norepinephrine. Clonidine slows norepinephrine production thereby halting many of the withdrawal symptoms. Naltrexone keeps any opiates from binding to the opiate receptors in the brain. This helps the patient from wanting to take the drug since no opiod receptor would be stimulated if one soon takes heroin. The clonazepan reduces anxiety and other medicines are also given to relieve nausea etc. Once this procedure is finished the patient still takes clonidine for a week or so and is put on a maintenance medicine of methadone or buprenorphine. Both of these medicines fit into and stimulate various opiod receptors but not the ones giving the patient the so-called "high" one receives from heroin. The other described detox program uses clonidine, buprenorphine, and clonzepan along with the usual drugs for nausea, pain, cramping etc. The buprenorphin does fit into certain opiod receptors making the patient feel somewhat better. Within days the patient is then put on naltexone, which prevents opiod binding to opiod receptors. The patient then receives maintenance medicines for a number of weeks. The maintenance medicines needed show just how hard it is for the patient to stay away from going back on heroin. Heroin addiction causes profound brain changes to many parts of the brain, which may take many years to get back to normal. Dopamine and endorphins must be secreted by the brain in their regular patterns and this takes time. Areas in the brain that deal with reinforcing behaviors have changed typically making the patient want to return to heroin. It can sometimes be difficult to stay on the methadone schedule and many patients learn they can abuse some of their medicines. Even with their maintenance programs patients typically experience negative changes in mood and feelings. Relapse occurs many times in many individuals and Switzerland has just now decided the best treatment is too just give addicts governmental supplied heroin doses. A funny thing about heroin is that this substance itself is not hard on the body. There is a case of an 84-year-old physician who was addicted to morphine for 60 years without any mental or physical problems. But of course heroin addiction is a nasty problem in which one typically must get the money to buy the drug. The potency of street drugs is always a big question mark and overdoses occur on a daily basis worldwide. This is indeed a drug to stay far away from. The lasting changes in the brain make for it a most difficult life for many individuals. It is best to just say no!

POPULATION BIOLOGY

We finally accomplished the feat by 1804. The world's population of humans finally made it to 1 billion humans inhabiting the earth at one time. It has been estimated that since

50,000 years ago approximately 106 billion humans have hung out on our earth. That's probably a tough statistic to positively back up but in our modern era we are much more adept in the field of statistics. We know the world's population reached 2 billion by 1927. We had around 3.5 billion by 1972 and by 1999 it reached 6 billion. In 2008 it is about 6.5 billion and is projected to reach 7 billion by 2012. By 2050 if the trend continues we will reach 9 billion humans goofing off on the earth at one time. These stats are very disturbing and sobering for a number of reasons. For one many of the so-called industrialized nations may actually see a decline in their populations. It is the so-called developing nations that are already stressed that will see high population surges. For example the United Nations expects that by 2050 Africa's population will rise from a current 900 million to almost 2 billion. Furthermore South Asia's population will go from 1.6 billion to nearly 2.5 billion. India now has over 1 billion individuals and by 2025 it is expected to have 1.395 billion. By 2050 it will contain somewhere around 1.593 billion in a country already having problems feeding the general population. China's population already over 1 billion will by 2025 be around 1.441 billion. We believe by 2025 that it is projected to decrease to 1.392 billion. Typical Indian women have an average of 3 children while China women average 1.7 children. The UN believes the population in the developing countries will go from 5.3 billion today to 7.8 billion in 2050. On the other hand the developed countries will remain unchanged at 1.7 billion. Europe's population is actually declining and is projected to go from the current 728 million to 653 million by 2050. This is pretty strange since about 2.2 million people immigrate to Europe every year. People in Europe are just currently having fewer babies. This also true of the United States but we will have a population increase mainly due to immigrants who tend to have more children. We of course have always been a nation of immigrants excluding the Native Americans who we have tended to destroy over the years in oh so many ways. We reached a population of 300 million in 2006 with about two-thirds of the population being made up of non-Hispanic whites. However the times will be changing for our country mostly due to the influx of immigrants coming into and staying in the United States. We will probably have around 400 million individuals by 2039. Over 1 in 4 residents is expected to be Hispanic which is now 1 in 7 residents. The number of Asians and Pacific Islanders will be around 28.3 million, which is more than twice the current populations. The African American population percentage is expected to stay the same, which is about 12% of the population. There will be a doubling of their population to 62 million by 2050 even though it will still be 12% of the population. It is expected that new immigrants and their descendents will account for 87% of the United States population growth between 2005 and 2050. So there will be major ethnicity changes to our population as we move through the 21st century. It will be interesting to see how we are able to respond to influx of change but it is obvious that a sound educational system will be needed. It will be essential that a sound home life will be needed with parents helping in the aspects of education. It will also require a revamping of society in general and many changes in governmental thoughts. Huge investments in our outdated infrastructure must be addressed which will provide jobs and security. Job opportunities must be made available to all members of our society or we will continue the decay of many of our societies. We will somehow have to adjust the growing change between the rich and the not rich. Currently our intelligence community is working on a "Global Trends 2025" report and it is already showing the United States dominance in the world will be much diminished. We will be seeing an economic rise in countries such China and other countries. Many organizations that have helped stabilize the world since World War II will become less influential. These may include the United Nations and the World Bank. We will have less control over other countries and may find that the billions of dollars pouring out of the United States for foreign aid may not be of much help to many nations. This has already been found to be true as the aid we give out to certain countries has been of little benefit. The report also offers the scary predictions that droughts, food shortages, and fresh water shortages will plague large swaths of the globe. The report also believes we have little to fear from other countries from an attack on us by conventional forces. We will have to somehow change our industrial - military complex, which will be exceedingly difficult to do. This of course is not to say that we should go back to an "isolationist" mentality. We need to adjust to the changes that will come in a positive way and work better with all world communities. This will be very difficult in many ways, as so many countries will have their own significant problems. Take India as an example. We are being told that India is on a progressive economic streak with many more Indians living the so-called middle class life. This is indeed true for millions of the people of India. For example, around 2001 many American companies found that they could outsource their call centers and information centers to India. India graduates many young eager students from universities. They are willing to work for cheap wages and they are quite intelligent. Typically working 50 or more hours per week they may earn between $2,500 - $4,000 dollars per year. Top pay in many high tech places may be only $30,000 - $40,000 per year. Of course this is big money in India. Unfortunately over 400 million Indians live below the poverty level and are still having kids. For many their houses are made with waste lumber, plastic sheeting, blankets, etc. Countless individuals live on the streets and even around rail lines. A slum called Dharavi in the city of Mumbai occupies only 520 acres. Unfortunately 600,000 humans live there and there is only 1 toilet for every 800 people. Over 500 million individuals earn only 1 dollar per day mostly working the fields or in sweatshops. Most of the roads are terrible and the buses and railroads are exceedingly crowded. Deforestation is rampant and will only get worse. Unfortunately this scenario is true for many of the other overcrowded countries of the world. The continuing expansion of their populations will be without a doubt one of the world's most vexing problems for the future. Global warming will most probably play a big roll in complicating an already complicated situation. We hope we win the battle.

PERHAPS VARIOUS SOLUTIONS EXIST

Our world is nowhere prepared for a large population increase especially as we humans now exist. Obviously many countries will be less distressed than others. For some population biologists a thinning of the herd may be our only saving grace. Asteroid or comet strikes might help but perhaps mankind itself may do the thinning for us. Or perhaps that nasty old influenza bug might be the ticket. Currently mankind is figuring out the DNA codes of the organisms of the world. DNA contains the code for making the proteins needed for the survival of each individual species. Even many viruses contain DNA although others contain what is called RNA. But RNA viruses must change their RNA code to DNA before they can grow and multiply. All bacteria contain only 1 chromosome that contains their specific DNA. If we have already not done so, scientists around the world will be able to devise new bacteria and viruses by rearranging DNA and adding snippets of DNA from other organisms. This may lead to many positives scientific feats. For example, we may produce a new bacterium that can digest sewage faster and more efficiently. That may seem kind of silly but overall the DNA rearrangements could have profound affects from a positive nature. We are already seeing this with some of the simple genetic rearrangements in crops and animal husbandry. However, evil may lurk out there in our infected world. We have feared attacks by the anthrax bacterium for a number of years yet it would not kill millions of humans. What is really needed to severely thin the herd would be an infectious air-born bacterium whose DNA has the code for producing a horrible protein poison. A good poison candidate would be ricin or a compound in its class. Ricin is one of the most poisonous proteins found in nature. It is produced by the castor oil plant (*Ricinus Communis*). This tall plant with huge star shaped flowers is a native of the tropics but grows as a weed all over the world. It is used as a decorative plant by many homeowners and it produces a large seedpod full of big fat seeds.

The seeds are very high in the poison ricin and have been known to cause human deaths. One to 3 seeds may be fatal to a child and 2 to 4 may kill an adult. 500 micrograms of the pure substance either inhaled or injected into a human may cause a horrible death. Of interest is that the world currently produces over 1 million tons of the seeds per year that are mostly made into the laxative castor oil. It is also used for lubrication in the motor industry. Of course in the making of these oils the poisonous ricin is removed. What makes ricin so poisonous is that upon entering the body it easily goes into our cells where it immediately begins to attack the ribosomes of our cells. The ribosomes are the protein factories of our cells producing the proteins the cell needs to survive. Without getting too specific the ricin destroys the ribosomes and within a couple of days the cells die. Unfortunately it is a slow and painful death from which modern medicine has no cure. The symptoms from poisoning may take 24 hours to show up with abdominal pain, vomiting, and diarrhea. The liver and kidneys start to fail and within a few days there is severe dehydration. One may experience burning throat, headache, shock, and shivering. Death comes with total exhaustion and intense cramping. That certainly sounds like a nice way to go! Of notable interest is that there also exists another poisonous plant protein that may be 75 times more deadly than ricin. It is known as abrin and is produced by the Rosary pea (*Abrus precatorius*). It mechanism of action is exactly the same as is found in the ricin protein. So here is perhaps a thought from some evil scientists. The DNA code for the castor bean plant or even the Rosary pea may soon be accomplished. Then it would be simple enough to find the gene, which is coding for the production of ricin or abrin. These scientists could ultimately replicate this genetic code and have it transferred into the DNA code of an air-born bacterium, which cases disease in humans. A couple of bacteria might be suitable candidates. One may be the very tiny *Micoplasma pneumoniae*, which causes primary atypical pneumonia. These bacteria only have a DNA coding capacity for only 700 proteins so it might be easy to attach the DNA code for making ricin or abrin to its DNA. Of course this is far from as simple as it seems but within years we will be able to readily alter bacteria and how they work. Ultimately these crazy scientists may be able to produce huge colonies of this bacteria that now have this horrible gene. This would be very difficult fortunately since they probably would have to be grown on living tissue. These bacteria do not survive long outside of humans. Somehow in this bizarre commentary these cultures would have to be sent into populated areas around the world and dispersed into the air. Humans would breath in the infectious bacteria that would then send their poisonous ricin or abrin proteins into the lung cells. Death would occur in days and before death they may possibly cough more bacteria in the air infecting others. Certainly this seems very far-fetched and somewhat futuristic but it is amazing what science is currently able to do. For example they may figure out a way so that this bacterium goes through its cellular divisions producing new organisms at a much faster rate. Could this possibly be a way to bring out a new and nastier form of the Black Death possibly killing off a significant amount of the human population? Only time will tell but it is on the minds of some sick souls as we speak. Now perhaps that scenario may be too much to believe but one knows that the bird flu of 1918 killed off a huge number of humans worldwide. Nobody knows the final tally since back then isolated areas existed everywhere. Perhaps 60 – 100 million humans died from this highly virulent strain of virus. That is a significant number since less than 2 billion of us were around at that time period. Influenza is caused by viruses that typically live in the digestive tracts of birds in the orient. Birds as they migrate tend to pass the viruses out in their wastes. When the wastes dry, the viruses become airborne and if they can enter the cells of the human respiratory tract they give us the flu. Viruses contain on their surface glycoprotein (sugar-protein) substances called hemagglutinins, which are spikes that attach to various receptors on our respiratory cells. If they can attach to these receptors then the virus enters the cell and uses our own cellular machinery to make more viruses. The cell ultimately blows up freeing the newly formed viruses to enter more cells to carry on the process. Viruses also produce a glycoprotein called a neuraminidase, which aids in blowing up the cell ejecting the viruses. We fight them off with white blood cells, antibodies, and protein substances called cytokines. Cytokines function to produce inflammations and to also destroy the viruses. Most likely all of us have had an episode of the flu and it is not fun. Our head hurts and our body aches throughout the ordeal. We may vomit and have episodes of diarrhea. But typically if we are a healthy individual we get better and soon forget about the episode. This however was far from the case of the flu of 1918. It is often called the Spanish Flu mostly due to the fact that Spain was one of the first countries to document its existence. It was caused by a bird flu whose subtype is H1N1. It is important to understand what H1N1 means in order to continue the story. Flu viruses produce 16 different hemagglutinin glycoproteins on their cell surface. An H1 virus produces a different one than say an H5 does. They also produce different neuraminidase glycoproteins like N1 or N2. Both of these glycoproteins can mutate in the viruses by changing the amino acids near their surface. These mutations may cause the virus to enter the cells of different organisms. For example most of the viruses that infect birds have hemagglutinin subtypes that allow the virus to only enter the lung cells of birds. Human flu viruses have hemagglutinin subtypes that easily enter certain human lung cells. Pig viruses (H3N2) typically have hemagglutinin subtypes that allow the virus to enter both bird and human lungs. Mutations are always occurring to the genes that code for hemagglutinin glycoproteins in viruses. This is why we cannot make a simple vaccination against the flu virus. This mutation issue was the cause for the flu virus of 1918 that killed so many people. Quite often a bird flu virus may get into pigs where it will mutate into a virus that can invade humans (swine flu). We do not think that is what happened to the avian (bird) virus of 1918. Scientists believe that a mutation occurred to the H1 glycoprotein and possibly the N1 glycoprotein allowing the virus to readily pass into almost all of the different types of lung cells in humans. A rapid reproduction of these viruses occurred spreading the viruses throughout the lungs. The victim's response was to activate their immune systems to fight off these viruses. But a weird and terrible thing occurred to many of these individuals with the flu. Their immune systems overreacted sending out huge amounts of inflammatory cytokines which function to kill the viruses. It is also believed that these viruses produced substances that kept the immune system from producing buffering anti-inflammatory compounds. So unfortunately for the victims their immune system spiraled out of control producing far to many of these protein cytokines. These cytokines in a matter of a day or 2 actually inflamed and destroyed their own lung cells through hemorrhaging. But what was also striking is that these victims also had hemorrhage from their mucous membranes of the nose, stomach, and intestines. This so-called "cytokine storm" destroyed many areas of the body but the lungs were especially destroyed. Death often came within a day or two. Of extreme interest is that a majority of the victims were young adults who typically have great immune systems. Well they did and this was actually the problem. Their immune system was able to go crazy since they were young and healthy. Older adults and even young children may have got the flu but their immune system did not work as well. They did not produce an extreme "cytokine storm" and so their own tissue was not ruined and they mostly survived. Currently we are worried about another pandemic flu striking us like the one, which occurred in 1918. With people now traveling all over the world it may theoretically be even worse since we have no cure for it. We had no cure then and most likely no cure for most of us this time. For the last 5 years or so a very nasty bird virus name H5N1 has been killings mostly chickens in the orient. The lethal rate approaches 100% and entire flocks have been destroyed if the virus is found in the area. It has also been lethal to other birds and even to tigers, which is real strange. Unfortunately it has also killed a number of humans who were in close contact with infected birds. Actually over 60% of the humans who have been infected have died. Of noteworthy interest is that the humans who have died have succumbed to the "cytokine storm" just like in 1918. Fortunately as of now the sick victims have not been able to pass this virus on to other humans. It is possible that the few infected breathed in large amounts of the virus or even that the viruses they took in slightly mutated allowing them entry into human lung cells. So in theory as long as the virus is not spread from people to people the world is good to go! However viruses do undergo constant yet somewhat random mutations. We are very worried that some slight genetic mutations to the hemmatoglutinin glycoproteins may make it possible for the virus to easily enter human lung cells. Another potential problem is that in China and Vietnam there exists in pigs an H3N2 swine flu virus. We are very worried that if the infected pigs take in the bird flu H5N1 virus a genetic exchange may occur. The H5N1 virus may pick up the pig genes changing its hemmatoglutinin glycoprotein structure so that it can easily get into human cells. So either way the potential for another pandemic like 1918 may exist in the future and the world is ill prepared for it. We have no good vaccinations and would have to produce literally billions of them in a short time anyway. Perhaps this will lead to a culling of the herd. By the way it may sometime soon be possible for mad scientists to mutate this beast in the lab and send it to the world. We shall ultimately see our fate whether it be good or bad AHMEN!

THE END FOR NOW

We are living in an incredibly interesting time in the history of the earth. We have the resources to dwell way back in the past and to study our histories. The scientific discoveries are becoming more fascinating every day. Our world is increasingly shrinking yet it is more complicated as societies become more intertwined. Yet we are still living in many ways as we have done for the lives of mankind. We seek food, shelter, contentment, and hopefully a satisfying life. We all know it is a short voyage and know nothing about a true afterlife. Albert Einstein did not worry about it at all. He realized with our simplistic existence that it is impossible to say what will happen upon death. He approached his death with the knowledge that the universe exists and perhaps forces beyond his understandings say it all. Most humans do have a faith in the future. Unfortunately for many this faith has led them into strange forms of organized religions. Organized religions have for years caused much of the world's problems mostly due to ignorance of the individual. Many believe "theirs" is the true way to go regardless of the logic of universal laws. We say for example this person is doomed to Hell due to the nasty deeds he performed in his life. Yet science is showing that our genetics and environment play a big role in our actions. We do not understand why bad things happen to good people and why good things may happen to bad people. Perhaps it is just the entropy of the universe making its mark. We constantly encounter random disorder and in many ways that is the way the universe functions. Perhaps upon death all of us good or bad will see a rearrangement in existence in which we can in no way comprehend at the moment. If it is just a lot of darkness and that is that well what can one say? Perhaps we should just say: "so it goes" and just try to lead a life that would make others proud.

SUGGESTIONS FOR FURTHER READING

Berkow, R. Ed. The Merck Manual. Rahway, N.J. Merck & Co. Inc. 1992

Stryer, L. Biochemistry. N.Y. WH Freeman and Co. 1988.

Weinberg, Gerald L. A World at Arms. Cambridge. Cambridge University Press. 1994.

Jenkins, Roy. Churchill A Biography. N.Y. Farrar, Straus, and Giroux. 2001.

Moyanahan, Brian. The Faith. N.Y. Doubleday. 2002.

Fox, Robin L. The Unauthorized Version. N.Y. Alfred A Knopf. 1992.

Stachel, John Ed. Einstein's Miraculous Year. Princeton NJ. Princeton University Press. 1998.

Dawood, N.J. Translator The Koran. London England. Penguin Books. 1990.

Wells, Spencer. Deep Ancestry. Washington DC. National Geographic Society. 2006.

Hamer, Dean. The God Gene. N.Y. Doubleday. 2004.

Churchill, W. The River War. N.Y. Award Book. 1964.

Irion, W.E. Ack-Acker. Self-published. 1990.

Pauling, Linus. How To Live Longer and Feel Better. N.Y. Avon Books. 1986.

Pauling, Linus. General Chemistry. N.Y. Dover Publications. 1947.

Gordon-Reed, Annette. Thomas Jefferson and Sally Hemmings An American Controversy. Charlottesville. University Press of Virginia. 1997.

Armstrong, Karen. Jerusalem One City, Three Faiths. N.Y. Alfred A Knopf. 1996.

Miles, David. The Tribes of Britain. Phoenix. Weidenfeld & Nicolson. 2005.

William, Winston. Translated. Josephus. Grand Rapids, Michigan. Kregal Publication. 1960.

Hawking, Stephen. The Universe in a Nutshell. N.Y. Bantum Books. 2001.

Jordan, Paul. Neanderthal. UK. Stutton Publishing. 2001.

Collins, Larry, Dominique Lapierre. Is Paris Burning. N.Y. Simon and Shuster. 1965.

Manheim, Ralph. Translator. Mein Kampf. Adolf Hitler. Boston. Houghton Mifflin. 1927.

Rossano, Matthew. Evolutionary Psychology. Southern Louisiana University. John Wiley & Sons, inc. 2003.

Green, Brian. The Fabric of the Cosmos. N.Y. Random House. 2004.

Brown, Stephen. Scurvy. N.Y. St. Martin's Press. 2003.

Diamond, Jared. Guns, Germs, and Steel. N.Y. W.W. Norton & Company. 1999.

Boorstin, Daniel. The Creators. N.Y. Random House. 1992.

Shirer, William L. The Rise and Fall of the Third Reich. N.Y. Simon and Shuster. 1960.

Garrett, Laurie. The Coming Plague. Plague, NY. Farar, Straus, and Giroux. 1994.

Pauling, Linus, Ewan Cameron. Cancer and Vitamin C. Philadelphia. Camino Books. 1979.

Randall, Willard, S. Randall. Jefferson A Life. N.Y. Henry Holt and Company. 1993.

Fernald, ML. Edible Wild Plants. N.Y. Harper & Row. 1943.

Made in the USA